ALEXANDRA WOOD

Alexandra Wood's plays include an adaptation of Jung Chang's *Wild Swans* (ART/Young Vic); *PIIGS:Spain* (Royal Court); *The Centre* (Islington Community Theatre); *Decade* (co-writer, Headlong); *Unbroken* (Gate); *The Lion's Mouth* (Royal Court Rough Cuts); *The Eleventh Capital* (Royal Court) and the radio play *Twelve Years* (BBC Radio 4). She is a winner of the George Devine Award and is currently the Big Room Playwright-in-residence at Paines Plough.

Other Titles in this Series

Alexandra Wood

THE EMPTY QUARTER

NICK HERN BOOKS

London

www.nickhernbooks.co.uk

A Nick Hern Book

The Empty Quarter first published in Great Britain in 2013 as a paperback original by Nick Hern Books Limited, The Glasshouse, 49a Goldhawk Road, London W12 8QP

Cover image: iStockphoto/ImageGap
Cover design: Ned Hoste, 2H

Typeset by Nick Hern Books, London
Printed in Great Britain by Mimeo Ltd, Huntingdon, Cambridgeshire PE29 6XX

A CIP catalogue record for this book is available from the British Library

ISBN 978 1 84842 366 4

The Empty Quarter was first performed at Hampstead Theatre Downstairs, London, on 26 September 2013. The cast was as follows:

GREG	Gunnar Cauthery
GEMMA	Geraldine Alexander
HOLLY	Jodie McNee
PATRICK	David Hounslow
Director	Anna Ledwich
Designer	Helen Goddard
Lighting	Lee Curran
Sound	Sarah Weltman

Thanks

I'd like to thank Clare Slater, Jack Lowe, Sarah Woodward and Hanna Jarman for their work on earlier versions of the play; Guy Jones, Alex Barron, Sacha Wares, Lyndsey Turner and Kat Wilkins for their thoughts on various drafts; Lisa, my ever-supportive agent; Ed, Greg, Will and everyone at Hampstead Theatre for the opportunity to get it in front of an audience; Anna and the whole team who have brought it to life.

A.W.

For the Cartwrights

Characters

HOLLY, *twenty-six in 2006*
GREG, *twenty-six in 2006*
GEMMA, *forty-nine in 2006*
PATRICK, *fifty in 2006*

The play takes place in Dubai between 2006 and 2011.

Note on Text

A forward slash in the text (/) indicates the point at which the next speaker begins.

A lack of a full stop at the end of a line indicates that the speaker cannot or does not want to finish.

This text went to press before the end of rehearsals and so may differ slightly from the play as performed.

ACT ONE

Scene One

2006. The living room of a Dubai apartment, twenty-two floors up.

GREG. Can give you a quick tour if you want.

GEMMA. I'll find my way around.

GREG. You sure?

GEMMA. They're all the same, these flats.

GREG. Well

GEMMA. Like what you've done with it though. These are nice.

GREG. From the market.

GEMMA. You got a deal I hope?

GREG. Can't remember what / we

GEMMA. How much?

GREG. I really can't / remember.

GEMMA. Takes a while to get used to the haggling.

GREG. We've been here a while.

GEMMA. Years, I mean. At first I thought a bit of flirting would do the trick, but they're wise to that, or maybe they never found me particularly appealing, what?

GREG. I didn't / say

GEMMA. If you want, in the future, if there's something you want, I'd be happy to go down there.

GREG. That's, thanks, / that's very

GEMMA. I'm sure you'll get the hang of it though.

GREG. I don't think it was / too

GEMMA. And it's all so much cheaper than at home anyway so, not that I'm up on how much things cost any more, but from what I hear it's just got more and more expensive.

GREG. I'll just show you / where

GEMMA. It's why a lot of people come out here.

GREG. What?

GEMMA. The cost of living back there. People get sick of it. Is that why you and Holly came?

GREG. I don't

GEMMA. And for the adventure of course, although she's probably had her fair share of that now.

GREG. I've got to go.

GEMMA. Of course you have, sorry.

GREG. She's not on any drugs but if she needs painkillers, they're in here.

GEMMA. And I don't need to

If she wants something she can have it, is that right?

GREG. Of course.

GEMMA. I just wanted to check there's not an issue with

But she'll take care of that herself, so that's fine.

GREG. I don't know what you've heard but

GEMMA. God no, I haven't heard anything, I just wasn't sure if

GREG. Obviously she was in a state when we found her, but she's fine now.

GEMMA. Of course, I'm just here to

GREG. Because you offered. And I'd rather she wasn't on her own, that's all.

GEMMA. Who wants to be on their own? A bit of company, that's all.

GREG. I wouldn't be leaving her if she was

She's fine, she'll tell you that herself, I mean, you'll see that.

GEMMA. That's excellent news, Greg.

GREG. I'm only going in, work've been pretty good, but I think they're reaching the limit of their understanding, so I'm going in, but I'll be back at seven-ish.

GEMMA. Perfect.

GREG. I could come back at lunch.

GEMMA. It's pointless, you'd spend the entire time in traffic, we'll be fine.

GREG. My office number's here, and this is my extension, if I'm not there, leave a message, or text. And if there was a problem or whatever, I could get back so just call me.

GEMMA. Greg.

GREG. I'm sorry if it's boring for you here all day.

GEMMA. Don't be silly.

   I brought a DVD, I hope that's alright.

GREG. Of course.

GEMMA. Is it alright to move the coffee table?

GREG. Yeah, I

GEMMA. Make myself at home, sorry, I do that, but it's *Six Week Six-Pack*. The DVD.

GREG. Haven't seen that one.

GEMMA. You wouldn't know anything about that kind of thing, not yet anyway, your abs are rock-hard without so much as a sit-up, but it's different when you get to my age, I won't scare you, but

   I'm on week five and feel. Go on, don't be shy.

   GREG *feels her stomach.*

GREG. Yeah, / it's impressive.

GEMMA. Nothing yet, but I didn't want to miss a day.

GREG. Not after five weeks.

GEMMA. Exactly. So I'll just need a bit of room in front of the telly, but I'll move it all back obviously.

GREG. I can move it now if you want.

GEMMA. No, no, it's all part of the training.

GREG. It's not too loud is it? The DVD.

Just, if Holly can sleep then it's probably good for her.

GEMMA. I'll keep it down.

GREG. And it's probably not the kind of thing she should be doing yet, so if she's

GEMMA. Understood.

GREG. I don't want to be over-the-top but

GEMMA. You're not being over-the-top, it's awful, what she went through. I mean, I don't know the ins and outs, obviously, but

GREG. Don't ask her questions.

Sorry, but I'd rather she focused on / something

GEMMA. You think I came to get the gossip?

GREG. No, I didn't mean / that.

GEMMA. If you think that then I can leave.

Pause.

GREG. I'm sorry, that's not what I think, Gemma, honestly, I don't.

I just hate the thought of people talking about her, not you, but people, and I know what people are like, they talk.

GEMMA. I'm not here for the gossip, Greg.

GREG. There is no gossip. That's the point, she's fine.

Just, just if she does start to talk about it, could you try to, I usually try to change the subject.

GEMMA. Maybe it's good to let her talk.

GREG. It doesn't help, so if she starts talking about it, just

GEMMA. Whatever you want. I'm a master of inane conversation, Patrick'll tell you that, it's my speciality, I can talk about the weather till the cows come home, it's in our DNA, right?

GREG. Thank you. Did I say that? Sorry, thank you. I do appreciate it, I really didn't want to leave her on her own. Not because she'd do anything, just because

GEMMA. It's lonely.

GREG. Yeah, well, yeah it is. It'll be fine when she gets a job but when you haven't got any friends around and

GEMMA. What am I?

GREG. Yeah, no, obviously you're a

Old friends, you know.

GEMMA. I'm old.

GREG. From uni and school, I mean.

GEMMA. I'm teasing, Greg.

GREG. Yeah, yeah, I know.

Just to, so you don't, she got a bit burnt out there, it's mostly healed, it wasn't permanent, she's not disfigured or anything, but that's what that is, and I don't want her feeling self-conscious about it, so

GEMMA. Shall I cover all the mirrors?

GREG. No, look, obviously she's seen it, I'm not, it's not a big deal, you'll barely notice it just

GEMMA. Don't stare.

It's sweet, Greg, it's very sweet that you care this much. I doubt Patrick would be this concerned if it was me.

GREG. If you want to order something in then give me the bill, I'll happily pay, it's the least I can do, and there's loads of fruit and veg in the fridge, so help yourself.

GEMMA. Fruit and veg.

GREG. Vitamins and minerals, I thought it'd be

GEMMA. British men have evolved since my day, I can tell you that. Patrick'd never eaten a vegetable that hadn't come out of a tin, when I met him, I'm not joking, he'd never seen corn on the cob.

GREG. Don't leave her.

She might say you don't need to be here and you can go, but please don't.

GEMMA. I promise. Scout's honour.

GREG. She can be very persuasive, / but

GEMMA. Were you a Scout? I bet you were.

GREG. No.

GEMMA. Neither was I, but I don't think that matters, I won't leave her, Scout's honour.

GREG. She says she doesn't need babysitting, but

GEMMA. Who's babysitting? Not me.

GREG. Okay, thank you, / that's

GEMMA. Off you go.

GREG. I'll be back as soon as I can.

GREG *heads to the door.*

GEMMA. No rush.

GREG. I've told her you're coming obviously, but just give her a few minutes when she wakes up, she's usually a bit out of it, always been like that, nothing to / do with

GEMMA. I'm the same. Don't worry.

GREG *exits.*

GEMMA *looks around the apartment.*

She looks in the fridge. She takes out an orange and smells it. She searches the drawers.

HOLLY *appears at the bedroom door, in her pyjamas. She watches* GEMMA *and waits for her to notice. Eventually* GEMMA *does.*

Holly.

Holly, hi, it's Gemma.

From the club. Gemma. How long have you been there?

I was just looking for a knife, but perhaps it's, it doesn't matter.

I fancied an orange, but I can peel it anyway, can't I, so

They smell amazing, have you had one? Let me peel one for you, they're packed full of Vitamin C, so good / for you.

HOLLY. What're you doing in my flat?

GEMMA. It's Gemma.

HOLLY. Why are you talking so loudly?

GEMMA. Am I? Sorry.

Greg asked me to, well no I offered, I offered to come and spend the day with you, we can do whatever you want.

HOLLY. Why are you going through my drawers?

GEMMA. I was looking for a knife. For the orange, like I said, but

HOLLY. Why can't you just peel it?

GEMMA. Well yes exactly, good point, and that's what I'll do.

Not a morning person. Don't worry, neither am I.

HOLLY. My jewellery's in the bedroom.

GEMMA. Jewellery? God no, I'm not after your

It's Gemma, Holly, I'm not a thief, I wasn't looking for your

I was looking for a knife, for the orange, it's Gemma.

HOLLY. You've said that five times.

GEMMA. You remember, don't you?

Married to Patrick, I'm, perhaps I look different, I'm not in my gym kit for once, do I / look

HOLLY. He's hidden them.

GEMMA. I'm not trying to steal your jewellery, Holly.

HOLLY. The knives.

GEMMA. Oh. Okay, well that doesn't matter, like I said, I'll just peel

She starts to peel the orange.

We don't / need

HOLLY. What've you done with my husband? He was here.

GEMMA. Yes, he was, but he's gone to work, the office, he's, you can call him if you like.

HOLLY. He wouldn't leave me, what've you done with him?

GEMMA *stops peeling and picks up a phone.*

GEMMA. Here, call him, I promise you he's fine, he just left, he

She picks up the phone and offers it to HOLLY.

Here.

HOLLY *smiles.*

What's

HOLLY *laughs.*

HOLLY. I'm sorry, Gemma, I'm sorry.

GEMMA. Oh, you're

HOLLY. Of course I know who you are.

GEMMA. Oh thank Christ.

HOLLY. I was messing with you.

GEMMA. I thought you were going to call the police.

HOLLY. I'm sorry, I shouldn't have.

GEMMA. No, it's

HOLLY. I've been so bored, like you wouldn't believe, and I just couldn't resist.

GEMMA. I thought God, I thought

HOLLY. It's Gemma, it's Gemma, it's / Gemma

GEMMA. I'm sorry, no, you had me, completely.

HOLLY. Married to Patrick.

GEMMA. I thought, I didn't know what would help, / I thought

HOLLY. I heard Greg and I just couldn't resist so I

GEMMA. I thought, Christ, she's gone crazy, I

Pause.

So I guess you're feeling better.

HOLLY. Nothing wrong with me. So what's the plan?

GEMMA. Plan?

HOLLY. I haven't seen anyone but Greg in five days. I need to get out of here.

GEMMA. I guess we could go to the club for a coffee or

HOLLY. Not there.

GEMMA. Or the mall, maybe, I

HOLLY. No.

GEMMA. What were you thinking?

HOLLY. I'll tell you what I want.

GEMMA. Go on.

Pause.

HOLLY. What's this exercise DVD you brought then?

GEMMA. Oh that was just in case you were asleep, keep me occupied, we don't need to do it.

HOLLY. I don't want you falling behind on your regime.

GEMMA. It's fine, I'll do an extra class tomorrow, don't worry about it.

HOLLY. I want to do some exercise.

GEMMA. It's not that good, I'm pretty sure it's not working so

HOLLY. There's nothing wrong with me, Gemma. It'd do me good.

GEMMA. No, no, I know that. Honestly, it's not great, I'm only sticking with it cos I started, but I won't be recommending it.

HOLLY. You think you're better than me, is that it?

GEMMA. No, no of course not, I just / don't

HOLLY. Don't want to show me up.

GEMMA. No it's

Well, I mean, I do do a lot of classes.

HOLLY. Brilliant, you can do a class for us here.

GEMMA. I don't lead them, I / just

HOLLY. It's just me, you can manage that can't you?

This is exactly what I need. Don't go easy on me though, alright?

GEMMA. Have you had breakfast? You should eat before we do anything.

HOLLY. All I've done is eat. I'll be fine. I'll get changed. And don't tell me you didn't bring your kit, cos I know for a fact you take it everywhere.

HOLLY *goes into her bedroom.*

Pause.

GEMMA. Did you want that orange?

GEMMA *peels the rest of the orange.*

She eats it.

HOLLY *enters in her workout kit. More of her skin is exposed, which reveals a slight burn on her arms and neck.*

GEMMA *notices her skin.*

HOLLY. It's cold in here, are you cold?

GEMMA. I'm okay.

HOLLY. Bloody air-conditioning.

She puts on a sweatshirt.

Doesn't matter, we'll warm up. Are you ready?

GEMMA. I'm not sure we should, Holly.

HOLLY. There's nothing wrong with me. I know what it is, Greg's told you I'm not allowed to do anything, but it's ridiculous. Look at me. Do I look like an invalid?

GEMMA. No.

HOLLY. I went for a walk in the desert and got a bit lost. Okay, so my navigational skills leave a little to be desired. Other than that

GEMMA. Did Greg tell you Marie and Carlos have gone home?

HOLLY. Yep, back to Chile, he told me.

GEMMA. Couldn't believe they'd been here five years. But, contract's up. She was a demon in the gym, did you ever do a class with her?

HOLLY *shakes her head.*

Brutal. I changed boxercise classes to avoid her.

HOLLY. Was she the tiny woman?

GEMMA. No, that's Valerie. She's Dutch.

HOLLY. Then I don't know who Marie was.

GEMMA. Yes you do. She spoke perfect English but when she got bored or didn't want to speak to you any more she'd switch back to Spanish and suddenly she couldn't understand a word you said. I mean it was shameless.

HOLLY. No.

GEMMA. You do, Holly, I know you've met her, we had a conversation, all three of us, when they started charging for the lockers at the club.

HOLLY. Can't think why I would've forgotten that.

GEMMA. You did meet her.

HOLLY. Okay, maybe I did, does it matter?

GEMMA. No, I guess not.

HOLLY. She's gone now anyway.

Pause.

You enjoying that?

GEMMA *nods.*

I'll prepare the space then, shall I?

HOLLY *goes to move the coffee table.*

GEMMA. Don't do it on your own, I'll help.

HOLLY. I can manage.

GEMMA. Let me help, it's heavy.

HOLLY. It's really not.

> HOLLY *pushes the table out of the way. She winces and holds her back.*

GEMMA. What've you done? What is it?

HOLLY. My back.

GEMMA. I told you to let me help, what did you do?

HOLLY. What am I, eighty? For God's sake it's a coffee table.

> *She picks up* GEMMA*'s bag.*

God, it's so heavy, I'm not sure I can hold it.

GEMMA (*taking bag*). Fine, you know what, you deserve what's coming to you.

HOLLY. That's the spirit. Get into your stuff. I'll choose the music.

> GEMMA *goes into the bathroom.*

> HOLLY *turns on some upbeat workout music. She starts to jump about.*

> GEMMA *enters in her gym kit.*

> (*Shouting over the music.*) I hate aerobics.

GEMMA. We don't have to do it.

HOLLY. No, I want to. Is this music okay?

GEMMA. Maybe we could

> GEMMA *turns it down.*

> HOLLY *starts doing star jumps.*

HOLLY. Let's do it, come on.

GEMMA. Okay, Holly, but let's just take it easy.

HOLLY. No chance.

GEMMA. For me, I'm old okay, so / just

HOLLY. Bullshit.

GEMMA. I'm not an instructor.

HOLLY. You're one hell of a procrastinator.

GEMMA. Fine.

> GEMMA *starts marching, bringing her knees up high, swinging her arms back and forth.* HOLLY *follows.*

HOLLY. What's this one called then?

GEMMA. The warm-up.

HOLLY. See, you know all the lingo.

> *They march.*

> Maybe that's where I went wrong in the desert, didn't warm up.

> When it's like fifty degrees you don't think you need to, but that's a rookie error, right? Anyone can tell you that.

> *They march.*

> Could've pulled a hamstring.

> Least I didn't do that.

GEMMA. Three two one.

> GEMMA *changes the exercise. Legs apart. She does squats.* HOLLY *follows.*

HOLLY. I've been meaning to get fit.

GEMMA. I do classes every day, you should join me.

HOLLY. No offence, but I hate the gym. I hate aerobics.

> GEMMA *stops.*

GEMMA. We can stop.

HOLLY. I don't want to stop. Keep going.

> GEMMA *starts again.*

> It's a means to an end, that's all.

GEMMA. I enjoy it.

HOLLY. But it is ridiculous, look at us. Objectively. What're we doing?

GEMMA. Squats.

HOLLY. We're kidding ourselves. We wouldn't stand a chance in the real world.

GEMMA. This is the real world.

HOLLY. I mean the jungle, the desert, nature, the real world.

GEMMA. You survived.

HOLLY. Barely.

GEMMA. One more.

They do one more squat. GEMMA *stands with her arms stretched out together above her head. She lifts her leg up and touches the toe with her hands. Then repeats it with her other leg.* HOLLY *follows.*

HOLLY. I want to go out there again.

GEMMA. This one's just like a standing crunch.

HOLLY. Have you and Patrick been into the desert?

GEMMA. Keep your legs as straight as you can.

HOLLY. Gemma.

GEMMA. Concentrate.

HOLLY. You must've been out there.

GEMMA. You should feel your heart rate going up now.

HOLLY. A desert safari, you must've done one of those.

GEMMA. Don't you want to do this properly?

HOLLY *concentrates on the moves.*

Two more.

GEMMA *changes the exercise. She stands with her hands behind her head and lunges forward, swapping the lead leg each time.* HOLLY *follows.*

HOLLY. If you haven't been I'll take you.

GEMMA. We've been.

HOLLY. I was trying to walk back.

GEMMA. Don't pull on your neck.

HOLLY. I was just trying to get back here.

GEMMA. You had cars, you didn't need to walk.

HOLLY. I left a note.

GEMMA. Chest up.

HOLLY. Why do you do this?

GEMMA. I told you, it's fun. We can stop if you don't like it.

HOLLY. Don't worry, I won't tell Greg.

GEMMA. Don't bend at the waist.

HOLLY. It'll be our little secret.

GEMMA. You said you felt okay.

HOLLY. I do.

I'm sure women hide worse things from their husbands.

GEMMA. Last one.

*GEMMA changes the exercise. She holds her arms in a
circle in front of her, and twists her body from side to side.*

HOLLY. Mum and I hid stuff from Dad all the time.

GEMMA. Don't open your arms.

HOLLY. Small things.

But it was fun.

They twist from side to side.

He might've felt left out.

If he'd noticed.

GEMMA. Five, four, three, two, one.

That's the end of the warm-up.

HOLLY. It worked, I'm warm.

She takes her sweatshirt off. GEMMA *notices her skin
again.*

GEMMA. So we can start with a knee crunch if you want.

She puts her arms above her head, then lifts her knee, and lowers her elbows to join it. She marches like this. HOLLY *follows.*

Does it hurt?

HOLLY. Not yet.

GEMMA. Your skin, I mean. The burn.

HOLLY. No.

GEMMA. I got so burnt on holiday once my parents had to take me to A and E. They were really angry.

I wanted to impress the pool attendant.

Spent the rest of the holiday in the room.

It healed though.

HOLLY. Exactly. No harm done.

GEMMA. Didn't get to kiss the attendant.

Greg must have been scared.

Four more.

They do four more. GEMMA *changes the exercise: backward lunges.* HOLLY *follows.*

When they couldn't find you, he must've been terrified.

HOLLY. Then they found me.

GEMMA. It's a miracle really.

HOLLY. Don't believe in miracles.

GEMMA. Very lucky then.

HOLLY. You're fit for a, how old are you?

GEMMA. Old.

HOLLY. Go on, I won't tell. Cross my heart.

GEMMA. Forty-nine.

HOLLY. Good.

GEMMA. What's good about it?

HOLLY. I didn't miss the big party we'll throw for your fiftieth.

They continue. GEMMA *stops for a moment.*

What's wrong?

GEMMA. Nothing, I just can't, what she does next. Burpees. That's it.

HOLLY. Excuse me.

GEMMA *does a burpee,* HOLLY *watches.*

GEMMA. Up and down. Back and stand.

Come on then.

HOLLY *follows.*

HOLLY. You should do something big for your fiftieth.

Everest. Kilimanjaro.

GEMMA. I'd be happy with a party.

HOLLY. I'm one for a challenge.

You should do one, you're fit enough.

GEMMA. On my own?

HOLLY. No.

GEMMA. Patrick wouldn't want to.

HOLLY. I'll do it.

GEMMA. Three more.

They do three more burpees.

GEMMA *starts squat rotations. Hands by her chest, she squats, then lifts her right knee and touches it with her left elbow. Alternates and repeats.* HOLLY *follows.*

HOLLY. Last time I was at the club.

Valerie, is it Valerie?

GEMMA. Dutch. Tiny.

HOLLY. Yeah, Valerie.

She talked about this bag she'd bought.

GEMMA. Yeah.

HOLLY. For half an hour.

GEMMA. Yeah.

HOLLY. Half an hour.

GEMMA. Yeah.

HOLLY. And then.

After half an hour.

GEMMA. Yeah?

HOLLY. She called me Louise.

They continue.

GEMMA. Louise left a year ago.

GEMMA *starts side lunges: arms above the head, legs apart and bend to the side, back to standing, repeat on other side.*

HOLLY. It's an amazing feeling.

GEMMA. Told you.

HOLLY. Walking out into all that space.

GEMMA. Weren't you scared?

HOLLY. I'm shit at these.

GEMMA. You don't have to go all the way down.

HOLLY. You are.

They lunge.

You'd like it.

You feel totally alive.

GEMMA. What about when you were lost?

When you ran out of water?

You could've died.

They lunge.

We have to lie down for the next ones.

They lie on the floor.

Stretch your right arm up, and your right leg down.

GEMMA *demonstrates a long-lever crunch, lifting her right arm and her right leg.*

HOLLY *follows.*

HOLLY. I want to do it again.

Make it all the way back this time.

I could do it. With some help.

GEMMA. Eyes up.

HOLLY. Someone to drop me. Pick me up.

GEMMA. You should talk to Greg.

HOLLY. He won't let me cut fruit.

GEMMA. Chin off your chest.

HOLLY. I need someone I can trust.

GEMMA. People train.

You can't just decide. Spur of the moment. To cross a desert.

Swap sides.

GEMMA *stretches her left arm and leg and lifts them.*

HOLLY. Not the whole thing.

Just a tiny bit.

GEMMA. Left side.

HOLLY *switches sides.*

You nearly died.

HOLLY. I felt alive.

Come with me. I'll show you.

GEMMA. I've been.

HOLLY. What are you doing on Sunday?

GEMMA. A class. Might see Julia. Can't remember.

HOLLY. Drive us into the desert.

GEMMA. It's too soon.

HOLLY. It'll be a reccy. That's all.

Music. Open road. Just us.

GEMMA. No wandering?

HOLLY. No wandering.

GEMMA *changes exercise. She goes into a press-up position, and starts doing plank jacks. Jumping her feet out and back to the centre again.*

So?

GEMMA. In out in out, come on.

HOLLY *follows.*

Scene Two

The same apartment. Weeks later.

GREG *is sitting at the table eating an Indian takeaway. He's listening to music at a high volume.*

After a while, HOLLY *enters.*

HOLLY. Didn't know we were having a party.

GREG. What?

HOLLY *turns down the music.*

HOLLY. Rave for one is it?

GREG. Watch this.

GREG *turns the music up, louder than it was.*

HOLLY. Yep, that's loud.

GREG *shakes his head and turns it louder.*

Okay, Greg.

GREG *shakes his head and turns it up to the max.*

What? It's loud, what?

She tries to turn it down but he won't let her. He lets it play for a while longer, then turns it off.

Yep, the speakers work.

GREG. I played it like that for twenty minutes.

HOLLY. Why?

GREG. I was waiting for someone to knock on the door and complain. No one did.

HOLLY. Quality walls.

GREG. We have the perfect neighbours.

HOLLY. Maybe they really like that song.

GREG. I wouldn't know, I've never met them.

HOLLY. Like you said, perfect.

GREG. You think that's perfect?

HOLLY. What were the names of our neighbours back home?

Anyone living in any of the flats. Go on.

Anyone.

GREG. Mr and Mrs MacFarland. Flat C.

HOLLY. What were their first names?

GREG. We had a formal relationship.

HOLLY. You had no relationship, Greg.

GREG. I know they were difficult to buy for.

HOLLY. Yeah, it's difficult to buy for people when you don't know them.

GREG. They had subscriptions to *The Economist*, *Time Out*, *National Geographic*, *Tate Magazine*. Obviously no one knew what to get them.

GREG eats.

HOLLY. Bad day?

GREG. Why?

HOLLY. Takeaway. Must be.

GREG eats.

All that saturated fat.

He stops.

GREG. It's a vegetable jalfrezi, with plain rice, I only do it once
in a while, I don't think it's going to / kill me.

HOLLY. Any for me?

GREG. Didn't know what you were doing.

HOLLY. At the club with Gemma.

GREG. There's enough.

HOLLY gets a plate from the cupboard.

Doing another class?

HOLLY. You know what she's like. I think she's got a problem
actually, bit obsessed.

She sits down and helps herself to the food.

Curry World?

GREG nods.

Julia was saying a new place opened. Spice Shack or
something.

GREG. Palace. You don't get shacks in Dubai.

HOLLY. Might be worth a try.

She eats.

GREG. Nothing beats Ravi's.

HOLLY. You're obsessed.

GREG. They do good curries, I'm not obsessed.

HOLLY. Other places are just as good, you just like to

You can't honestly tell the difference between this and one of theirs.

GREG. Course I can.

HOLLY. Well I can't.

They eat.

GREG. How's the job hunt?

HOLLY *shrugs*.

Anything interesting?

HOLLY. Few things.

GREG. Like what?

HOLLY. I'm applying, Greg, don't worry, I know you want me slaving away.

GREG. Not slaving / away.

HOLLY. Joke.

GREG. It'd be a good way to meet people as much as anything.

I don't want you doing something you don't want to do.

HOLLY. Right. Could do that at home, so

What'd be the point.

GREG. Anything caught your eye?

HOLLY. Do you want a list or

GREG. I'm not checking up, it's just, do you think there will be? Is that why

I mean, is there something you think you might want to do that you could only do here?

HOLLY *shrugs*.

It's a fair question isn't it?

HOLLY. Yes, it's a fair question.

GREG. So?

HOLLY. I don't know.

> What do you want me to say? I want to become a world expert in a rare desert rat, only found here, what do you want?

> *She eats.*

GREG. Mike emailed. Said he might visit in May.

HOLLY. Be nice. You could take him sandboarding, he'd love that.

GREG. Might bring Jackie.

HOLLY. Who's Jackie?

GREG. His fiancée.

HOLLY. His what?

GREG. Yep.

HOLLY. Jackie? Who's

GREG. Yep. Seems really into her. Well, loves her, he said. Asked her to marry him, he's never done that before, so

HOLLY. Mike's getting married?

GREG. Yeah.

HOLLY. That won't last.

GREG. That's nice.

HOLLY. Come on, it's Mike.

GREG. So?

HOLLY. It's probably just an excuse to have a stag do. Actually, no, this is probably an excuse to get you back there, for the stag do.

GREG. I just told you he said he's coming out here so

HOLLY. You seen a picture?

> GREG *nods.*

> And?

GREG. What can you tell from a picture?

HOLLY. Loads.

GREG. I didn't even know he was seeing someone and now he's getting married.

HOLLY. Well our engagement was pretty sudden, doesn't / mean he was

GREG. That's different, your mum was ill, we had to move faster than we / might've done.

HOLLY. Well maybe they've got reasons for moving fast too. Maybe she's pregnant. That'd make sense.

GREG. He told me he's getting married in an email.

HOLLY. It's Mike.

GREG. Yes, exactly.

HOLLY. He probably proposed in an email.

GREG. No. He did it properly. Down on one knee and everything.

HOLLY. When's the next rugby tour?

GREG. March.

HOLLY. Yeah, well let's just see if it survives that.

GREG. Just another thing I'll miss out on.

HOLLY. You could go.

    He asked you to be best man yet?

    GREG *shakes his head.*

    He will.

GREG. In an email?

HOLLY. Why don't you organise something with the guys from work for Friday?

    You like them.

GREG. I've only known them five minutes.

HOLLY. I'm only talking about dune bashing or something Greg, you don't have to have their babies.

GREG. They're fine, but they're not

HOLLY. We're only twenty-six. Is that it, we're not going to make any more good friends?

GREG. Of course we can make new friends, I just

HOLLY. Mike's getting on with things, good for him. You can't expect people to stay exactly the same.

GREG. I don't.

HOLLY. You do.

GREG. I moved here didn't I?

HOLLY. Yeah. Things were going to change anyway, whether Mike gets married or not.

GREG. I get it, I just miss them, that's all, I'm allowed to miss them aren't I?

Don't you?

HOLLY. What's the point?

GREG. There is no point, I can't help it.

HOLLY. Try.

GREG. We have good friends. At home. Family.

HOLLY. Some family.

GREG. Some. We had jobs, it's not like we couldn't get jobs.

HOLLY. We've got friends here.

GREG. People we know, yeah.

HOLLY. You have a job.

GREG. We both had jobs at home.

HOLLY. We have a flat.

GREG. I tried to get in the wrong one today.

HOLLY. The wrong flat?

GREG *nods*.

HOLLY *laughs*.

GREG. It's not funny.

HOLLY. It's quite funny, Greg, come on.

GREG. It was the same flat, same position, just wrong floor.

HOLLY. How much had you had?

GREG. Nothing.

They all look the same.

HOLLY. Shhh, you're not allowed to say that.

GREG. Feels like we're living in a hotel.

HOLLY. Can think of worse places to be.

GREG. This isn't somewhere you live.

HOLLY. What are we doing then?

GREG. I don't know. That's what I'm

I don't really know.

Pause.

HOLLY. We're having a good time, aren't we? We're

GREG. Where were you today?

HOLLY. With Gemma, I told you.

GREG. At the club?

Pause.

We haven't even been married two years, Holly, and you're already lying to me.

HOLLY. I'm still entitled to some privacy / aren't I?

GREG. Gemma told me she drove you into the desert.

HOLLY. She what?

GREG. She was worried. She told me she only did it a few times, how you'd asked her to stop, but she thought you might still be going out there. Is that true?

HOLLY. Some friend.

GREG. She thought I should know. As your husband, she
    thought I had a right / to know.

HOLLY. Play us against each other.

GREG. Is it true, Holly?

HOLLY. Gemma says, must be.

GREG. I'm asking you.

HOLLY. It's not a big deal.

    Pause.

GREG. If it hadn't been for your mum, do you think we still
    would've got married?

HOLLY. Yes.

    Eventually. Would've taken you an age to ask, but we
    would've.

GREG. Do you even want me here?

HOLLY. What kind of question is that?

GREG. Do you?

HOLLY. Yes.

GREG. Then why are you spending all your time on your own,
    wandering in the desert?

    Pause.

HOLLY. The guy from the car park drives me. Drops me off.

GREG. What guy?

HOLLY. Rohan.

GREG. The parking attendant?

HOLLY. He's nice. I pay him a little, not much, but he's got
    four kids back in Pakistan / so he's

GREG. Why, Holly?

HOLLY. Training.

GREG. For what?

HOLLY. Better to be prepared, isn't it?

GREG. Training for what, Holly? A race? The Apocalypse? What?

HOLLY. Just

GREG. Extreme Scouting?

HOLLY. No just

GREG. Bit old for the Scouts.

You could go to Exmoor, the Peak District, there are places you can train back home if that's what you want.

HOLLY. This is the most hostile desert in the world.

GREG. I know.

HOLLY. I want to cross it.

GREG. Cross it?

HOLLY. Some of it.

GREG. I could barely get you to go for a walk on the Heath before.

HOLLY. This is different.

GREG. Yeah, there's a serious chance you could die. I heard a thing yesterday, two guys driving across the desert, caught in a sandstorm, buried alive. Is that what you want?

HOLLY. Of course not.

GREG. Then explain it to me, because I don't get it.

HOLLY. I can't explain exactly, all I know is I want to cross it.

GREG. Is that why we had to come out here?

HOLLY. It's not the worst place in the world, Greg, it's

GREG. It's not home.

HOLLY. What's so great about home? Look what happens at home.

Pause.

I want to know that I can, that I did that, whatever happens.

GREG. What's going to happen?

HOLLY. Anything can happen. Mum died. That's what's going to happen, everything and anything but if I can do this then

If I can cross a desert, if I can survive that

Then, that's something.

Pause.

GREG. Okay. So talk to me.

It's good, if you've got a goal, that's good. But why do you have to do it in secret? Why'd you have to sneak around?

HOLLY. You didn't want me doing it.

GREG. I don't want you being reckless, but we could do it together, train together, safely, get some advice rather than just wandering

HOLLY *shakes her head.*

Why not?

HOLLY. I have to be able to do it on my own.

GREG. Who says?

HOLLY. I need to know I can.

GREG. We're supposed to be partners. That's what I'm here for.

HOLLY. And what about when you're not?

GREG. I'm here now.

Let's cross the desert. Let's go all Lawrence of Arabia. Let's hire some camels. Are camels allowed or do you want to do it all on foot?

I'll be the perfect travel companion. I won't ask if we're nearly there yet. I won't go on about my blisters. I won't speak slowly and loudly in English to the natives. I won't call them natives. Are we allowed to call them natives?

HOLLY. I need to do it on my own, Greg.

GREG. Why marry me if you want to do everything on your own?

I know we got married sooner than we would've, to make your mum happy. But maybe having me there helped you a bit. Maybe it wasn't the worst thing.

Pause.

I quit my job.

HOLLY. What?

GREG. I quit.

If you can walk into the desert, if it's alright for you to walk into some hundred-degree oven and to keep on doing it even though you nearly died then I can quit my job, can't I?

HOLLY. You quit to get back at me?

GREG. No.

HOLLY. We've got a flat to pay for, you can't just quit.

GREG. So we'll sell it.

HOLLY. You're the one that bought it.

GREG. Because I thought that's what you wanted.

I bought it for you. Everything I do is for you.

HOLLY. Not everything, Greg, you didn't quit your job for me, did you?

GREG. At home I did.

Pause.

HOLLY. Have you got another one in mind?

GREG. It wasn't the job.

HOLLY. I'm just starting to settle in and

GREG. We've never met our neighbours, I'm not sure they even exist.

HOLLY. Of course they exist.

GREG. My best friend's marrying a woman I've never met. Our so-called friends here sell us a flat we didn't even want. That's not settling in.

I've given it a go, Holly.

HOLLY. You can't just give up.

GREG. Why not?

HOLLY. What kind of attitude is that? Where's that going to get us?

GREG. Home.

HOLLY. No.

GREG. No?

Pause.

I want to go home, Holly.

I tried. I gave it a go, didn't I?

HOLLY. We've only been here five minutes.

GREG. I'd stay here longer if I thought there was any chance of sharing anything with you.

HOLLY. You could've talked to me about it.

GREG. I didn't want to chicken out.

I can't say no to you. How I ended up here, isn't it.

HOLLY. We'll never be able to afford a place like this at home.

GREG. You think that's why I came here? Property.

HOLLY. We won't be here for ever.

GREG. Bet that's what Patrick and Gemma said.

HOLLY. We won't.

GREG. I don't want to be here at all.

Come home with me.

HOLLY. Not yet.

GREG. I'm serious, Holly. I'm going home.

HOLLY. You're not asking?

GREG. I'm asking you to come with me. I want you to come with me. But I am going home.

HOLLY. You're leaving me?

GREG. No, I'm asking you to come with me. If you won't then

Then I guess you're on your own.

ACT TWO

Scene One

An apartment, twenty-nine floors up, which looks the same as the other one.

HOLLY *sits alone at the table. She's wearing the same clothes as in the previous scene, although she looks worse for wear now.*

She picks at the food in the Indian takeaway cartons on the table.

GEMMA *enters from the bathroom.*

GEMMA. Sorry about that, you caught me off-guard. It's great to see you though.

Oh God, don't eat that, it's been sitting there all night. I'll get you something if you're hungry.

She stacks up the rubbish.

I wasn't expecting

We're not usually takeaway types. Usually out and about. I did ask Patrick to clear up, you'd think he could manage that wouldn't you, but apparently not.

Spice Palace, it's the new place, have you been?

HOLLY *shakes her head.*

It's alright.

She bins the rubbish.

What can I get you? A juice or something?

GEMMA *looks in the fridge.*

We've got tomato juice. For the Bloody Marys really, but, is that okay?

HOLLY *nods.*

And then to eat, it's looking a bit grim I'm afraid, not like
your fridge, overflowing.

GEMMA *pours her a glass of tomato juice and hands it
to her.*

Let's go out for some food.

HOLLY. I'd rather not.

GEMMA. Oh, okay, well, um, there's not, I'm not sure what
we can

HOLLY. Can I have a shower?

GEMMA. A shower? Yes, of

Is that the new thing? You don't go for coffee now, it's
a shower.

HOLLY *smiles*.

Check up on what shower gel we're using.

I think we're on Molton Brown at the moment, hope
that's okay.

HOLLY. I haven't got anything with me.

GEMMA. You can borrow a towel, that's not a problem.

HOLLY. Just need to freshen up.

GEMMA. Are you alright?

Don't look like you've had much sleep.

HOLLY *shakes her head*.

Out partying all night? Why wasn't I invited?

I'm joking.

GEMMA *gets a towel*.

They're Suvin cotton, have you tried it? So much better than
Egyptian. Feel how soft that is.

HOLLY *touches the towel and nods*.

Has something happened?

She sips the tomato juice.

Is it Greg? Have you had an argument or something or

It's normal, you know.

Pause.

He hasn't, God, he didn't

HOLLY. What?

GEMMA. Hit you. Did he?

HOLLY. Do I look like a battered wife?

GEMMA. You never know what goes on behind closed doors, you hear terrible stories, people you wouldn't expect. If he has

You wouldn't be the first, Holly, and it's nothing to be ashamed of, / it

HOLLY. He'd never do that.

GEMMA. Fine. But if he did

HOLLY. Do you wish he had?

GEMMA. Why on earth would I wish that?

HOLLY. Good bit of gossip.

GEMMA. Is that what you think of me? If I'm such a gossip go and ask one of your many friends for a shower, Holly.

HOLLY. I'm sorry.

GEMMA. What's going on?

Is it the plumbing? We've had some trouble. These places go up so fast there are bound to be problems.

Let's go for a class. You can shower at the club after.

HOLLY *shakes her head.*

Why not?

HOLLY. Can't.

GEMMA. A bit of exercise would do you good. Release those endorphins.

HOLLY. I can't go there.

GEMMA. Course you can, you're not barred are you?

HOLLY. Probably.

GEMMA. Why would they bar you?

HOLLY. If you can't pay.

GEMMA. You can pay.

Pause.

Oh.

You know Patrick and I can always help out if you're a bit short.

HOLLY. Worse than that.

GEMMA. It's easy to get carried away here. It happens to everyone.

HOLLY. What happens?

GEMMA. Overspending now and again, it's not a problem.

GEMMA *gets her wallet and takes out a wad of notes.*

Here. What do you need?

HOLLY. More than that.

GEMMA. Okay, how much more?

Pause.

How much more, Holly?

HOLLY. They arrested him.

GEMMA. What?

HOLLY. Greg.

GEMMA. Why? What happened?

HOLLY. He quit his job.

GEMMA. He quit?

HOLLY. The bank froze his account, wouldn't pay the mortgage.

They've locked us out of our flat, we can't get in there, all our stuff's still in there, our clothes, our, everything. They arrested him, they held him like he was a rapist or something, I told them we'd pay, but they didn't even give us a chance.

GEMMA. When did this happen?

HOLLY. Two days ago.

GEMMA. Two days? Where've you been since then?

HOLLY. The car. Rohan let me but / then they

GEMMA. Who's Rohan?

HOLLY. The attendant.

GEMMA. In the car park?

HOLLY. He let me sleep in there, but then they found me and they fired him. He's got a wife and four kids back home, he was only being kind by letting me stay there he

GEMMA. Okay, calm down. Firstly, I'm glad you told me. I'm glad you came here. You should've come here immediately, I don't know why you / didn't, but

HOLLY. What can I do? Gemma, what do I do?

GEMMA. It'll be alright.

HOLLY. He'll go to prison. Greg. None of this is his fault.

GEMMA. Why did he quit?

HOLLY. He wants to go home.

GEMMA. And you?

HOLLY. What's that matter now?

GEMMA. You can't just up and leave like that.

HOLLY. I'll tell him that, shall I? If I see him again, I'll mention it, thanks.

GEMMA. Of course you'll see him again, Holly, you need to calm down.

HOLLY. What am I supposed to do? Who do I speak to? You must know people, Patrick must know people.

GEMMA. You're in shock.

HOLLY. I'm not the one in some medieval prison cell right now.

GEMMA. No, you're here.

And you'll stay here.

I won't have you living in a car park. You can stay as long as
you need.

HOLLY. What about Greg?

GEMMA. We'll do everything we can.

HOLLY. He can't be the first, this must've happened to other
people.

GEMMA. Worst case, prison.

HOLLY. It's fucking Dickensian.

GEMMA. It's the system here.

HOLLY. It's fucked up.

GEMMA. It isn't the same as home. But what did you expect?

HOLLY. We're not criminals. I didn't expect to be treated like
criminals.

Pause.

GEMMA. Have you spoken to your family?

HOLLY *shakes her head.*

Maybe you shouldn't. For now. Until there's more to tell
them. There's not much they could do, and it's not as if
you're on the street.

What about people here? Do you need to call anyone, let
them know?

HOLLY *shakes her head.*

No one?

HOLLY. He should never have bought that flat.

GEMMA. It was a good investment.

HOLLY. For who?

GEMMA. For the both of you of course. Who else?

HOLLY. I doubt your husband did too badly.

GEMMA. It was Greg's decision to buy it, Holly, Patrick hardly had a gun to his head.

HOLLY. Do they allow visitors? Can I see him today do you think?

GEMMA. I don't know the prison visitors' schedule. I've never needed to go.

HOLLY. I need to see him.

GEMMA. We will.

HOLLY. It's my fault. He thought it's what I wanted. The flat.

GEMMA. Wasn't it?

HOLLY. You hear stories. People caught having sex on the beach, and you think, fair enough, won't do that, we'll be alright, but that's nothing.

GEMMA. Let me order some food, you haven't eaten.

HOLLY. What'll Greg be getting?

GEMMA. I'm sure they'll feed him.

HOLLY. Really?

Just so I could go wandering in the desert.

GEMMA. Blaming yourself isn't going to help.

HOLLY. What will? Tell me, cos I have no idea.

GEMMA. Breakfast.

HOLLY. I don't think so.

GEMMA. What're you going to do on an empty stomach?

HOLLY. I'm not hungry.

GEMMA. You say that, but when you smell the almond croissants from Le Café, have you had those?

HOLLY. What?

GEMMA. I know I shouldn't, the cholesterol, but special occasions.

HOLLY. It's not exactly a birthday is it.

GEMMA. Now and again, that's what I mean, and I think we could both do with some carbs.

Do you want anything more substantial? Sue tells me their baguettes aren't bad.

HOLLY. I can't eat.

GEMMA. Are you sure because I could call them now.

HOLLY. Do they use torture in these places?

GEMMA. God no.

HOLLY. This is exactly the kind of place they'd use torture.

GEMMA. Not with debtors.

HOLLY. Electric shocks, waterboarding, God / knows.

GEMMA. Come on, Holly, he's not a terrorist.

HOLLY. Do they have the death penalty?

GEMMA. Not for people like Greg.

HOLLY. But they have it?

GEMMA. For murderers, drug dealers, people like that.

HOLLY. You don't know.

GEMMA. I've lived here a long time.

HOLLY. But you don't know, do you, you can't honestly tell me they wouldn't

He didn't even want to be here.

GEMMA. Why don't you have a shower?

HOLLY. While Greg's being tortured?

GEMMA. You have to wash, Holly, and you have to eat. You might not feel like it, but these things have to be done. You can borrow my clothes. I'm guessing you don't have any.

HOLLY. Neither does he, he's got nothing.

GEMMA. We'll go and buy you some.

HOLLY. I haven't got any money.

I literally have nothing, I don't even have my wallet, not that my cards would work, but I don't even have that, I don't have change for a coffee, I couldn't even buy a fucking latte.

GEMMA. I'll get them.

HOLLY. You don't have to buy me clothes.

GEMMA. You don't want to be wearing mine.

HOLLY. I'm hardly in a position to be worrying about how I look.

GEMMA. And you're not really in a position to be turning away help either.

Pause.

HOLLY. I'm sorry.

GEMMA. Don't apologise. I'll buy you a few tops, some underwear, that's all.

HOLLY. That's very generous but

GEMMA. I don't want you feeling uncomfortable about it.

HOLLY. Well I would.

GEMMA. Surely it's better than wearing my pants?

My old granny pants.

Pause.

If you'd rather, I could drop you at another friend's.

HOLLY. I came here didn't I?

GEMMA. We're in the same building. It was convenience, wasn't it?

HOLLY. I still have the car, could've driven anywhere.

GEMMA. Why didn't you then?

HOLLY. Because I thought you'd

I wanted to come here.

GEMMA. Did you? Haven't seen you in a while.

At first I thought it was me, but no one at the club's seen you either so

HOLLY. I didn't want to inconvenience you.

GEMMA. I thought maybe you didn't like my music, it's probably a bit old.

I knew it couldn't be my driving though, I happen to know I'm a good driver, I've never once had an accident in twenty years and that's a miracle as far as this place is concerned, Patrick's written off three cars.

I know you kept going out there.

HOLLY. Rohan drove me.

GEMMA. The attendant?

HOLLY *nods*.

And you trusted him?

HOLLY. And now he's lost his job because of me.

GEMMA. He could've left you out there, driven off with the car, disappeared.

HOLLY. He wouldn't have done that.

GEMMA. It was a risk wasn't it?

HOLLY. He risked his job to help me.

GEMMA. I helped you, didn't I?

HOLLY. You told Greg.

GEMMA. Only because I was worried about you.

I was worried you were going out there, and I was right, wasn't I?

I shouldn't have, you're right. But you're here now, and I can make it up to you.

I'm glad you're here. You were right to come.

Patrick can be pushy, doesn't take no for an answer. It's not a criticism, he's done very well, but he could probably have made it clearer to Greg, the situation here in terms of debt. It's zero tolerance really.

HOLLY. We should've known, it's not Patrick's fault.

GEMMA. Still, I feel

HOLLY. Don't.

GEMMA. But stay with us, we'll make up for it.

HOLLY. You don't have to make up for anything.

GEMMA. It won't be too strange though, will it?

HOLLY. What?

GEMMA. Sleeping here.

HOLLY. I'm not the one sleeping in a cell.

GEMMA. It's almost exactly the same as your flat.

HOLLY. Greg always said it felt like a hotel.

GEMMA. Don't think of it as a hotel, while you're here, it should feel like your home.

Why don't you start with a shower.

She hands HOLLY *the towel.*

HOLLY. I want to go to the station.

GEMMA. We will, but have a shower first.

HOLLY *takes the towel.*

And choose whatever you want from my wardrobe.

HOLLY. These'll be fine.

GEMMA. Nonsense, I'll give them a wash and you can have them back.

You know where the bathroom is.

HOLLY *goes into the bathroom and shuts the door.*

Just pass me your clothes and I'll wash them now.

She waits outside the door.

Holly?

HOLLY *passes her clothes to* GEMMA *through a crack in the door.*

GEMMA *puts them in the washing machine.*

The sound of the shower.

GEMMA *tidies up.*

Scene Two

The same apartment, a few weeks later. Music is playing loudly. HOLLY*'s wearing some of* GEMMA*'s gym kit. She's vacuuming.*

GEMMA *enters and turns off the music.* HOLLY *continues to vacuum.*

GEMMA. Quite loud, Holly.

We have neighbours.

Pause.

Holly?

HOLLY *looks up.*

What're you doing?

HOLLY. Cleaning.

GEMMA. Why?

HOLLY *continues to vacuum.*

You don't have to do that.

Holly.

GEMMA *pulls the plug out of the socket. The vacuum stops.*

HOLLY. I haven't finished.

GEMMA. You don't have to do that.

HOLLY. I know. I want to.

GEMMA. You shouldn't be doing that.

HOLLY. Why not?

GEMMA. You're a guest / here.

HOLLY. You said to treat this like my home. I clean my home, so

GEMMA. Is it not up to your standards?

HOLLY. I'm staying here, Gemma, it's the least I can do, cleaning is the least I can do.

GEMMA. We have Tala for that.

HOLLY. Is it a problem that I'm doing a bit of vacuuming, helping Tala out, is that really such a big problem?

Pause.

GEMMA. What's wrong?

HOLLY. What could possibly be wrong?

I just want to do something, anything, I can't sit around.

GEMMA. Let's go to the club then, shopping, but not this.

HOLLY. Why not?

GEMMA. It's Tala's job.

HOLLY. You don't let me cook, you don't let me clean, you don't / let me

GEMMA. Most people would be happy / not to have

HOLLY. I need to do something.

GEMMA. Let's drive into the desert then. How about that?

I can drive you out there, like before.

HOLLY *shakes her head.*

You can choose the music.

You let some car-park attendant drive you, but not me.

HOLLY. I don't want to go out there.

GEMMA. All of a sudden.

It was all you could think about before but now

HOLLY. Things have changed a bit.

GEMMA. Well, yeah but

I mean, I understand why you don't like going to the club and the malls and, but you wouldn't have to see anyone out there, I would've thought you'd like that, I would've thought it was perfect.

HOLLY. Can I just finish the vacuuming?

GEMMA. Greg wouldn't expect you to stay inside the whole time.

HOLLY. I was nearly done.

GEMMA. One minute you're risking everything to go out there and the next

HOLLY *pushes the plug back into the socket and the vacuum starts. She continues to vacuum the room.* GEMMA *watches her.*

That's a new tracksuit.

I don't appreciate you cleaning the flat in my new tracksuit, Holly.

Wear your own clothes if you insist on cleaning.

Scene Three

The apartment, a few days later. The sound of the shower.

HOLLY *stands in the kitchen area, meticulously preparing a Bloody Mary. She's wearing the same clothes* GEMMA *was wearing in Act Two, Scene One.*

She finishes preparing the drink and cleans up the minor mess, going beyond what's necessary in the already pristine kitchen.

PATRICK *enters.*

HOLLY. Evening, Patrick.

PATRICK. You see this is why I don't have a dog.

HOLLY. Are you allowed / dogs?

PATRICK. Second you come in, it's the eyes and the wagging tail.

HOLLY. I just made you a drink.

She holds up the Bloody Mary.

I won't say anything.

He puts his things down and takes the drink.

He sits on the sofa, loosens his tie and sips the drink.

Pause.

PATRICK. It's good. Cheers.

HOLLY. I've got the hang of it now I think.

Gemma just jumped in the shower.

She wants to head out for dinner.

PATRICK *nods.*

Pause.

Long day?

PATRICK. Is this you not saying anything?

HOLLY. Sorry.

PATRICK. Feel free to get on with whatever you were

HOLLY. Saw Greg today.

PATRICK. How was he?

HOLLY. Not good.

PATRICK. Sorry to hear that. There's a lot wrong with this place. But nowhere's perfect.

Pause.

HOLLY. It's not in a room or anything. The visit. He stands one side of this fence, and I'm the other side. Of a different fence. They're like, three metres apart.

PATRICK. It's not good.

HOLLY. No, it's not.

I can't touch him.

PATRICK. I don't know what to tell you, Holly.

HOLLY. All I want to do is hold him.

PATRICK. You're better off talking to Gemma, she's better at this kind of thing.

HOLLY. I don't want sympathy.

PATRICK. Good, well, that's good.

I'm just not the sympathetic kind.

HOLLY. No room for sympathy in business.

PATRICK. That could be true.

HOLLY. I get that.

PATRICK. You're a perceptive girl.

If we're going out, I'll take this opportunity to have a quick ten winks.

PATRICK *shuts his eyes.*

Pause.

You can sit there by all means, but

HOLLY. I've got nothing to do.

PATRICK. Lucky you.

HOLLY. Not really.

PATRICK. You weren't working before.

You must've filled your time somehow.

HOLLY. I did but

PATRICK. So?

HOLLY. It usually involved spending money.

PATRICK. Ah.

Pause.

HOLLY. I'm not a scrounger.

PATRICK. No one would think that of you.

HOLLY. I hate it. Scrounging.

Pause.

PATRICK. Gemma tells me you've been doing the cleaning.

HOLLY. Once. I did it once.

PATRICK. We have Tala.

HOLLY. I know but, I just needed to do something, to occupy myself.

PATRICK. So we'll fire her then.

HOLLY. What?

PATRICK. If you're going to do her job there's no point keeping her.

HOLLY. It was only once.

PATRICK. You can see my point can't you?

Pause.

Gemma doesn't like you cleaning. I don't see the problem myself, my mum was a cleaner, I have no problem with you scrubbing our toilet. But I also feel for Tala. If we fire her, she'll have nothing, whereas you, you have something, even when you have nothing. You don't know the meaning of nothing.

You stop. Tala keeps her job. It's simple.

HOLLY. So I can't even clean now?

I was just trying to do something useful, I don't want Tala to lose her job because of me.

PATRICK. It's a perverse kind of place, but here we are.

Pause.

He shuts his eyes again.

The sound of the shower stops.

HOLLY. Gemma will be ready soon.

PATRICK. Thanks for the commentary.

HOLLY. I just wanted to talk / to you.

PATRICK. I don't rate education, Holly. I know you've got one, and that's nice for you, but I deal with educated people all day and most of them are idiots.

All day. Every day. Idiots.

I'll tell you what I do rate. Intelligence. Intuitive intelligence. Can you see where this is going?

HOLLY. I know you're tired.

PATRICK. Good. Maybe you have some, Holly, one of the lucky few.

HOLLY. But I wanted to talk to you while / we're alone.

PATRICK. Maybe not.

HOLLY. I want to talk about a business matter. In private.

PATRICK. I've finished work for the day.

He closes his eyes again.

HOLLY. A businessman's never off-duty, is he?

PATRICK. This one is.

HOLLY. Please.

Pause.

PATRICK. What do you want, a written invitation? Go on then.

HOLLY. Are you going to open your eyes?

Pause.

Okay, fair enough. I wanted to ask if you'll pay off our debts. If you'll loan us the money, that is, to pay off our debts. It would only be a loan. We'd work out an interest rate to make it worthwhile for you. Of course. It's a business proposition.

Pause.

PATRICK. Why wouldn't you want Gemma to hear?

HOLLY. It's not a secret, it's just

It's a business proposition, and

PATRICK. You said that.

HOLLY. So, that's why I've come to you.

Pause.

Could you open your eyes do you think? Sorry, it's just this is serious, I'm serious.

PATRICK *opens his eyes.*

PATRICK. And I'm seriously tired.

HOLLY. Is it something you'd consider?

PATRICK. What about your parents?

HOLLY. Dad's got his new life, why should he bail us out? And Greg's family couldn't help anyway, so what's the point in worrying them?

PATRICK. They don't even know what's happened?

HOLLY. We'll tell them when it's sorted. But we got ourselves in this mess

PATRICK. And I'm supposed to get you out of it?

I'm not a bank, Holly. I don't know what you've heard, but

HOLLY. You're successful. Self-made. That's what I've heard.

I admire that.

PATRICK. I am pleased you approve.

Pause.

HOLLY. We're graduates, / and I know

PATRICK. So you're already in debt.

HOLLY. Whatever you think of the merits or not of education, statistically we're more likely to get jobs / and earn

PATRICK. Which you'll then quit, when it suits you.

HOLLY. Statistically, graduates earn more over the course of their / careers.

PATRICK. What statistics?

HOLLY. Patrick, I promise you'll get your money back. And more.

We'll do whatever job we have to.

PATRICK. Even cleaning?

HOLLY. Whatever we need to do.

PATRICK. Need to do more than that to pay back that kind of money.

GEMMA *comes out of the bathroom.*

GEMMA. Give me twenty minutes.

Must be nice having a beautiful young woman handing you a drink when you walk through the door.

PATRICK. I'm a lucky man.

GEMMA. Don't you forget it.

There's a new Japanese I thought we could try.

PATRICK. I hate Japanese food.

GEMMA. It's good for you.

PATRICK. I don't enjoy it.

GEMMA. We'll go with the majority. Do you like it, Holly?

HOLLY. I thought I'd stay in tonight. Let you two have some time alone.

GEMMA. How many times have I told you, we've had twenty years alone.

You have to eat.

HOLLY. All I seem to do is eat.

GEMMA. You're not getting out of it that easy. You like Japanese, don't you?

PATRICK. That's a leading question, isn't it?

GEMMA. Holly?

HOLLY. It's fine.

GEMMA. Right, decision made.

HOLLY. I like most food, it doesn't have to be

GEMMA. I want to try it. They say it's the new Imperial Sushi, we'll see about that.

PATRICK. I hate that place.

GEMMA. We're not going there.

Fifteen minutes.

GEMMA *goes into her bedroom and shuts the door.*

HOLLY. Sorry, it's just she's seen me eating sushi.

Pause.

Greg can't stay there. I have to do something. If it was Gemma, wouldn't you

PATRICK. I'd never let that happen.

HOLLY. I know you don't do sympathy.

This is just business.

PATRICK. It can't be.

You're living in my apartment. You and my wife are friends.

HOLLY. We are, but

PATRICK. But?

HOLLY. We've only known each other, what

PATRICK. Long enough she invited you to live here.

HOLLY. Just until

I'm grateful, of course I am, God knows where I'd be if it wasn't for the two of you / but

PATRICK. Gemma. If it wasn't for Gemma.

HOLLY. But you don't want me living here permanently.

PATRICK. So now you're blackmailing me.

HOLLY. What?

PATRICK. Bail me out or have me here forever. You're forgetting a third option. We could just ask you to leave. We could have nothing more to do with you.

HOLLY. Gemma wouldn't do that.

PATRICK. You're right.

Some people'd find it a burden, having you here. But then they wouldn't have invited you. Gemma enjoys it, she's social, she likes playing the hostess.

So why deny her that opportunity?

HOLLY. I'm not here to entertain her.

PATRICK. You'll move back home when Greg gets out.

HOLLY. I don't know.

PATRICK. Of course you will.

HOLLY. I honestly don't know.

It'd be completely official, Patrick, we'd draw up a contract and a repayment plan. We'd start paying it back as soon as he's out.

PATRICK. You can't promise that, you don't even know where you'll be.

I'm not a bank.

HOLLY. You've done well here.

PATRICK. I'm not a charity either.

HOLLY. We're not asking for charity. At five percent interest, say, over fifteen years you'd be making nearly sixty-seven thousand pounds. Tax-free. That's hardly charity.

PATRICK. You've done your maths.

HOLLY. I've had nothing else to do.

PATRICK. Five percent?

HOLLY. Say.

PATRICK. What've you got in terms of security?

Property? A car? Your degrees, I suppose.

HOLLY. The contract. We'd be legally / bound to

PATRICK. So you go bankrupt, where am I then? What guarantee would I have, Holly?

Without security you'd have to be offering far more than five percent.

HOLLY. We could negotiate that, of course, if it's something you'd be

PATRICK. Ten percent, at least.

HOLLY. That's, we can negotiate, if it's something you'll consider, then

Is it?

Pause.

In fifteen years, say, you'll be coming up to retirement, sixty-seven thousand pounds would come in handy wouldn't it?

PATRICK. How do you know when I plan to retire?

HOLLY. Sixty-seven thousand, at any time, that's pretty good.

PATRICK. I told you, at five percent, I'm not interested.

HOLLY. At ten percent you'd be getting, that'd be double what you'd be lending us.

PATRICK. You're the one that's come to me.

Pause.

You know why Tala came here?

HOLLY. To work.

PATRICK. To support her family. She can't just quit when she wants to go home.

You know how long since she's seen her two kids?

HOLLY. A long time, I imagine.

PATRICK. Three years. Can you imagine that?

HOLLY *shakes her head*.

You get to visit Greg at least.

She came here because she had to and she stays here because she has to.

If I was going to help anyone, why not start with her?

HOLLY. Because she could never pay back the loan with a hundred and forty grand of interest.

PATRICK. There's no guarantee you can either.

GEMMA *enters*.

GEMMA. I was going to say, if you want to choose something to wear for dinner, Holly, then

HOLLY. I'll be alright, thanks.

GEMMA. You sure? It's just, I don't usually wear that for dinner.

HOLLY. Is it smart, this place?

GEMMA. I've never been, but

HOLLY. I don't really feel like / dressing up.

PATRICK. If she doesn't feel like it, Gemma

GEMMA. If you don't like anything I've / got then

HOLLY. It's not that, I'm just not really in the mood / to go

GEMMA. It wouldn't hurt to change, would it?

PATRICK. If they turn us away we'll just have to go elsewhere.

GEMMA. That'd suit you, wouldn't it?

Look, it's up to you, the offer's there, that's all.

HOLLY. Thank you.

GEMMA *goes back into her room.*

PATRICK. Do you like it here?

HOLLY. With you?

PATRICK. Dubai.

HOLLY. I can see why it appeals to people.

PATRICK. But not you?

HOLLY. It's alright.

PATRICK. Don't lie to me.

If you want to do business, don't lie to me.

HOLLY. What, you don't think it's alright? You're the ones who've been here twenty years.

Pause.

It's hard to be enthusiastic about the place when Greg's in prison.

PATRICK. Tell you what I miss. Old-man pubs.

Don't know where I'll drink when I'm an actual old man.

HOLLY. Won't you go back?

PATRICK. Planned to, but

Pause.

Sixty-seven thousand pounds would pay for a few nurses to wipe our geriatric arses I suppose.

HOLLY. You've got a few years before you have worry about that.

PATRICK. But I do have to worry about it. Ultimately.

Pause.

What if Greg worked for me?

HOLLY. He wants to go home.

PATRICK. I loan you the money. Five percent interest. But Greg works for me.

HOLLY. Here?

PATRICK. Where else?

HOLLY. For how long?

PATRICK. However long it takes. Fifteen years?

HOLLY. Fifteen years?

PATRICK. You could live well out here while you paid it back.

HOLLY. We never planned to be here that long.

PATRICK. Did you plan for Greg to go to prison?

Plans change.

HOLLY. He doesn't know anything about construction.

PATRICK. I'd find him a suitable position.

HOLLY. Like what?

PATRICK. IT skills are always an asset.

HOLLY. What if we didn't want to stay?

PATRICK. It's just one solution, Holly. No pressure. If you've got others, feel free to pursue them.

HOLLY. You know we haven't.

PATRICK. You have. You could call your dad. Or Greg could serve his sentence.

HOLLY. And where would I stay, while he did that?

PATRICK. I don't know what you expect, but I'm not going to hand over a hundred and fifty thousand pounds and watch you fly off into the sunset.

GEMMA *enters*.

GEMMA. Zip.

PATRICK *zips up her dress*.

Well?

PATRICK. Very nice.

GEMMA. It was in the sale, wasn't it, Holly.

HOLLY. What?

GEMMA. The dress. The sale.

HOLLY. Yeah.

GEMMA. She was more enthusiastic in the shop. Convinced me to get it.

HOLLY. It's nice.

GEMMA. I can take it back.

PATRICK. You look good, keep it.

GEMMA. Does it fit alright?

PATRICK. Perfect.

GEMMA. So you're not changing?

PATRICK. Give her a minute.

GEMMA. I've booked the table for eight.

PATRICK. She's a bit distracted.

GEMMA. Look I know seeing Greg must be hard, but that's why it's good for you to get dressed up and come out with us, take your mind off it.

PATRICK. Holly was telling me what it's like. The fences.

GEMMA. You haven't been interrogating the poor girl? There's no point dwelling on it. It is what it is.

PATRICK. It doesn't have to be.

GEMMA. Saying things like that doesn't help.

PATRICK. Holly has options.

GEMMA. Her husband's in jail, Patrick, they're limited.

PATRICK. Not if I pay off their debts.

GEMMA. Go and change your shirt.

PATRICK. Holly's come up with a business arrangement that could benefit us all.

HOLLY. I need time to think.

GEMMA. You pay their debts?

PATRICK. It could work out. I loan them the money, and they pay it back with interest of course.

GEMMA. That's a lot of money, Patrick, are / you sure

PATRICK. Have I ever let you down?

GEMMA. I'm not questioning your ability to / provide.

PATRICK. Alright then.

GEMMA. Just that, because she's a friend, because we're close to them, your judgement might be

You didn't talk to me about it.

HOLLY. I didn't know we had to share everything.

GEMMA. We spend all day together and it never came up?

And you just decide to spend hundreds of thousands without even consulting me.

HOLLY. Nothing's been decided, Gemma.

PATRICK. Since when do I run my business decisions past you?

GEMMA. This is different.

It's because you saw him today, I can understand why you might panic, but you've got somewhere to stay, and the time will pass and he'll be out before you know it.

PATRICK. If he makes it out.

GEMMA. Why would you say that?

PATRICK. You hear stories, these places aren't holiday camps, there's no hiding it. How many men does he share with?

GEMMA. Patrick.

PATRICK. They're not all debtors, I can tell you that.

GEMMA. He looked alright, didn't he? Today. You said he looked alright.

PATRICK. Across two fences, what can you see?

GEMMA. He was standing, you said he looked pretty good, considering.

PATRICK. If you have the choice, all I'm saying, is if you have the choice, why would you leave him to rot in that prison?

GEMMA. People don't choose / prison, Patrick.

PATRICK. You're taking a risk that he'll be okay. If he gets out, he won't be the same man. Can't be.

Pause.

HOLLY. Could we take holidays? Go home for holidays?

PATRICK. He'd be an employee, not a slave. He'd get annual leave.

GEMMA. What are you talking about?

PATRICK. You'd have weekends, evenings together, you could have a family if that's what you want, you'd be living your lives.

HOLLY. Here.

PATRICK. There are worse places.

GEMMA. What's going on?

PATRICK. Well? What do you say?

GEMMA. About what?

PATRICK. I've offered Greg a job. As part of the agreement he'd work for me.

GEMMA. Here?

PATRICK. Do I have offices anywhere else?

GEMMA. You'd be staying here?

PATRICK. For the repayment period. Fifteen years maybe.

GEMMA. Fifteen.

　　We've benefited, Holly, from being here, we'd never have all this back home. You can establish yourself here, in ways you never could there. And it takes time. People come and go but they don't get the best out of the place. Fifteen years, you could.

HOLLY. I need to speak to Greg / before I

PATRICK. Of course.

GEMMA. Do you really think he'd rather be in prison?

PATRICK. Speak to him, of course.

GEMMA. This calls for a celebration.

PATRICK. Nothing's been agreed yet.

GEMMA. We'll get dressed up, try out this Japanese, go for drinks. I've got the perfect dress.

HOLLY. I have to speak to / Greg before

GEMMA. You'll love it.

GEMMA *rushes into her bedroom.*

PATRICK. I think it's a good solution.

GEMMA *emerges, holding the dress.*

GEMMA. Isn't it gorgeous?

HOLLY *nods.*

(*Hands it to her.*) Here, put it on.

HOLLY *takes the dress.*

(*To* PATRICK, *as they go into the bedroom.*) Wear the pink shirt tonight, I always love you in that.

Scene Four

The apartment, weeks later.

GEMMA, HOLLY *and* GREG *enter.*

GEMMA. Here we are, now what can I get you? Cup of tea?
   Beer? A shower, a bed, God there must be so many things
   you've missed. Must want to do everything all at once.
   Anything.

HOLLY. Maybe a beer?

GREG. Yeah.

GEMMA. Poor man's overwhelmed. Must be completely
   overwhelming.

HOLLY. Do you want to sit down?

GREG. I'm not sick.

GEMMA. Good to hear it. You hear stories, people coming out of
   those places with God knows what. Flea-infested I'm sure.

GREG. You can burn my clothes if you want.

GEMMA. I'm sure that won't be necessary, but thank you.

GREG. Here.

   GREG *takes off his shirt.* HOLLY *stares at him.*

   I don't want to infect your flat.

GEMMA. You don't need to worry about that, really.

GREG. I don't want it, here.

HOLLY. Greg.

GEMMA. No it's okay, I'll take it.

   GEMMA *takes the shirt and puts it in the bin. She washes
   her hands.*

   You can borrow something of Patrick's.

GREG. Would you like me to?

GEMMA. You might feel more comfortable, that's all.

   He's got plenty, they'll be a little big, but

Holly, show him Patrick's wardrobe. Choose whatever you want.

I'll get you a drink, what would you like? Sorry, a beer, you said.

HOLLY *shows* GREG *the bedroom. He goes in and shuts the door.*

GEMMA *opens a bottle of beer.*

He looks well. Considering.

HOLLY (*through the door*). Are you alright, Greg?

GREG *enters, now wearing an old, washed-out football shirt and shorts.*

GEMMA. My God, where'd you find that?

GREG. The wardrobe.

GEMMA. Probably more flea-ridden than yours was.

GREG. Fits.

GEMMA. Used to fit Patrick, can you believe that?

He was a good-looking man, believe it or not. Been enjoying the good life for too long, that's his problem.

HOLLY. Doesn't sound like a problem.

GEMMA. Are you a fan?

GREG. Football?

GEMMA. More of a rugby man I bet.

HOLLY. Played a bit at uni, didn't you.

GEMMA. I knew it. Patrick refuses to watch, won't miss the football, follows that, but won't watch rugby, even the Six Nations, patriotic things like that, refuses.

GREG. Football, not rugby. Good to know.

GEMMA (*passes him the beer*). Here. Holly?

HOLLY. I'm okay.

GEMMA. We can't let Greg drink alone, not today, go on.

GREG. Go on, Hol.

HOLLY. Fine. A beer.

GEMMA. I'll join you.

>GEMMA *gets two bottles of beer from the fridge and opens them.*

Beer's not really my thing but

GREG. It's a special occasion.

GEMMA. Should be champagne really, but we'll save that for later.

>*She hands* HOLLY *a beer.*

Anyway, cheers. Welcome home.

>*They raise their bottles and drink.*

Should've offered you a glass, do you want one?

HOLLY. We'll manage.

GEMMA. What am I talking about, you rugby types aren't precious, are you. Rugby boys at university used to drink from bins, God knows what was in them. Used to go and cheer them on. How is it?

>GREG *smiles.*

As good as you remember?

GREG. It's good.

GEMMA. You'll want to call your parents of course.

>After your beer perhaps.

GREG. Priorities.

GEMMA. God, that sounds terrible, doesn't it. Call them now if you want.

HOLLY. One thing at a time.

GEMMA. Sorry, I get overexcited. You might have noticed that. Holly knows.

>*They sip their beers.*

Holly's been in the spare room, so obviously you'll both be in there for a while, until you're back on your feet.

HOLLY. We haven't had time to talk about it yet.

GEMMA. Of course.

HOLLY. Haven't had a minute alone so

GEMMA. Patrick's looking forward to working with you.

GREG. When do I start?

GEMMA. Obviously you'll need time to recover, before he starts cracking the whip / but

HOLLY. Are you going to your class this afternoon?

GEMMA. Thought I'd stick around, in case you needed anything.

HOLLY. I know where everything is, you can go.

Promise we won't burn the place down.

GEMMA. God knows what skills he picked up in there.

GREG. Didn't meet any arsonists. Don't think it's complicated though.

GEMMA. I suppose not. I'll hide the matches shall I?

HOLLY. It's boxfit today, you should go.

GEMMA. I don't miss a class for much, Holly knows.

HOLLY. You never miss a class.

GREG. I'm honoured then, you'd miss it to babysit us.

GEMMA. Not babysit.

HOLLY. Exactly. We don't need babysitting. You should go.

GEMMA. Holly's been coming with me, while you were away.

Wasn't keen to start with, think it's fair to say, but you're feeling the benefits now, aren't you?

Why don't we all go?

HOLLY. Greg doesn't feel up to it.

GEMMA. He's already in the kit.

> It's more strenuous than you might think though, Holly'll tell you.

HOLLY. We'll stay here.

GEMMA. I understand. Lots of catching up to do. It's just, it makes sense, since we'll be at the club anyway.

HOLLY. When?

GEMMA. Eight-ish.

HOLLY. Tonight?

GEMMA. Bit of a celebration.

GREG. That's nice.

GEMMA. I thought so. Patrick'll be there.

HOLLY. We'd rather be alone tonight.

GEMMA. Right, no, of course.

> Don't want to disappoint Patrick though.

HOLLY. Probably sick of the sight of me.

GEMMA. Don't say that, he loves having / you here.

HOLLY. It's just one night alone, Gemma. Is it such a big ask?

GEMMA. Normally, no.

HOLLY. Normally?

GEMMA. It's just, there might be a few others there as well.

HOLLY. Who?

GEMMA. Friends.

HOLLY. How many?

GEMMA. I don't know exactly.

> People wanted to welcome Greg home, what was I supposed to say?

HOLLY. That you'd ask him. Us.

> That on his first night he might want to take it easy.

GEMMA. He's young, he can handle a few drinks, can't you?

GREG. If you think so.

HOLLY. Greg.

GEMMA. Well, no, Greg, it's not about me, it's only if you want to.

GREG. You tell me.

GEMMA. I can't tell you how you feel, but it's only people you know, it'll be nice.

GREG. I'm yours, Gemma, you're in charge.

HOLLY. I just want to spend an evening alone with my husband.

GEMMA. People were shocked by what happened to you. They just want to see you're alright, now you're out, that you're okay.

GREG. If it'll make them feel better.

GEMMA. Obviously it's not about them, you're the one that's been through it, but, I know they'd love to see you.

HOLLY. Did any of them visit him?

GEMMA. It was difficult enough for you to get in, Holly, be fair.

HOLLY. Fair?

GEMMA. Look, I don't want to make a thing of it, but I've told people you'll be there.

HOLLY. That's not our fault.

GEMMA. No, but

    I guess I did get a bit overexcited. You know me, I can't help myself, and before you know it there's a cake and music and / dancing.

HOLLY. There's a cake?

GEMMA. It's low-fat, don't worry.

HOLLY. It's not his birthday.

GEMMA. I know, and if you think it's inappropriate we can scrap it. Forget the cake, but people will still be there, / and

HOLLY. They can celebrate without us.

GEMMA. Look, I just thought it'd be good for you.

HOLLY. For us?

GEMMA. Yes.

Now I think about it properly it's completely overstepping the mark, I should've asked.

HOLLY. Yes.

GEMMA. I know none of this is what you wanted, I know that, I'm not stupid.

It's going to take time to adjust to this whole situation. But you're going to find it easier if you just throw yourself into it. If you join a rugby team, Greg, and you do more classes at the club, Holly, and you go for drinks after work, all that stuff. You might not feel like it, but it helps. It's the only way, really.

I know you think of me as the wicked stepmother, and that's okay. Look you don't have to come.

GREG. We'll come.

GEMMA. You don't have to, honestly.

GREG. We'll come.

GEMMA. I don't want you coming just to humour me, this crazy lady, no one would be surprised if you / weren't

HOLLY. One drink.

GEMMA *smiles*.

ACT THREE

Scene One

2011. An apartment, almost identical to the previous two.

GEMMA. Can I come in then?

GREG. You've just caught me, I'm heading off, Gemma.

GEMMA. Bit late aren't you?

GREG. Why are you here?

GEMMA. For Holly of course.

GREG. She's actually, she's got someone coming round so

GEMMA. Monique. I know.

   I told her not to worry.

GREG. You told Monique not to

GEMMA. I told her I was coming anyway, there's no need for
   both of us to be here, is there.

GREG. You told her not to come?

GEMMA. There's no need.

GREG. Do you think that was

   I mean, actually Holly was looking forward to seeing her.

GEMMA. Oh for goodness' sake, she sees her all the time.

GREG. She sees you all the time.

   Pause.

GEMMA. Are you going to let me in then?

   Pause.

   What's wrong, Greg?

GREG *lets* GEMMA *in*.

She was grateful, to be honest, said she had things to do. I thought I was helping.

GREG. She offered to come over. Just yesterday.

GEMMA. Something must've come up, what can I say.

GREG. She only spoke to Holly yesterday.

GEMMA. Look I don't know, Greg, does it matter? As long as someone's here with her.

You don't need to stand on ceremony. Get to work, go on. You're late. Need to earn all you can now, babies are expensive commodities.

GREG. They're not commodities.

GEMMA. Got out the wrong side of bed this morning, didn't you.

GREG. Didn't sleep much last night.

Holly's just got to sleep now, so if you wouldn't mind letting her

GEMMA. She's only pregnant, Greg, it's not

Women have been managing it for thousands of years so there's no need to get all

GREG. She's tired. Just asking you to let her sleep, that's all. Don't think that's too indulgent, is it?

GEMMA. It's good for pregnant women to keep as active as they can.

GREG. It's also good for them to sleep.

GEMMA. Listen to us.

Talking as if we're experts.

What would we know.

Pause.

GREG. Thanks for being here.

Think she's finding it difficult, you know, without her mum to talk to.

So it's nice to have some company.

GEMMA. Did you hear about Darren?

GREG. No.

GEMMA. Thought you were friends.

GREG. What about him?

GEMMA. Played Sevens with him, didn't you?

GREG. What happened, Gemma?

GEMMA. Fled the country, didn't he.

GREG. What?

GEMMA. You didn't hear?

GREG. When?

GEMMA. Few days ago. Just upped and left. Don't know what he thinks he's going back to.

GREG. He didn't say anything.

GEMMA. He's hardly the first. Abandoned cars all over the place, people just get out while they can. Better than prison I suppose. Well, you'd know better than anyone.

GREG. I knew he was struggling to find something.

GEMMA. It's worse back there.

GREG. He didn't even say goodbye.

GEMMA. We'll miss him. Worked for Patrick ten years. One of the family.

Not nice having to let him go but what can you do? No one's indispensable, I guess that's what you learn.

Least he didn't have kids, that's something.

HOLLY *comes out of the bedroom.*

GREG. You're awake.

HOLLY. Sort of.

GREG. Monique

Monique couldn't make it, last minute. So Gemma kindly came round instead.

HOLLY. Oh.

GEMMA. Have to make do with me I'm afraid.

HOLLY. No, that's

Thanks.

Are you missing a class though?

GEMMA. I can do one tonight, it's no problem.

Perhaps we can do a gentle workout here, don't worry, Greg, gentle.

HOLLY. I'm pretty tired to be honest.

GEMMA. Well, we'll see.

GREG. Just take it easy.

GEMMA. If you want to get to the office before lunch you should probably

GREG. Yeah, I better go.

He kisses HOLLY.

Just give me a call if you need anything.

GEMMA. That's what I'm here for, now go.

GREG. I am.

I'll be back as early as I can.

GEMMA. You do everything you need to. We'll be fine.

GREG *exits*.

He's a worrier isn't he.

HOLLY. It's sweet.

GEMMA. He'd have you lying in bed like an invalid if he had his way. You're only pregnant, I was trying to explain to him, women do this every day. Tala would've told you, she had her kids and she was back to work the next day.

HOLLY. She probably wouldn't have chosen that.

GEMMA. We fuss and we / pamper

HOLLY. We?

GEMMA. Western women, we make a fuss, but really, the body knows what it's doing, it's nature, it's designed to do this, / there's

HOLLY. Still

There are things you can do to help. Eat the right things, / rest

GEMMA. Have you had breakfast?

HOLLY. I'll have something later, I'm feeling queasy.

GEMMA (*going to the kitchen area*). Probably because you're hungry, I'll make you something.

HOLLY. It's because I'm pregnant, Gemma.

GEMMA. Some fruit.

HOLLY. I really couldn't stomach it.

GEMMA. Vitamins and minerals. Baby needs those doesn't it.

HOLLY. Later.

GEMMA *takes an orange from the fridge. She takes a knife.*

HOLLY *sits down.*

Pause.

GEMMA (*cutting the orange*). I was fond of Tala.

Miss her. You think I'd be used to losing people by now.

But we'd talk. I taught her English. Bits and bobs, you know, but I enjoyed it actually. She was a fast learner, or maybe I was a good teacher. No, she was very smart.

Still, you can't be sentimental about these things, can you.

No one's indispensable, no matter how close you are. And it just wasn't necessary to keep her on.

She understood.

She puts the orange pieces on a plate and takes it to HOLLY.

Here you go.

HOLLY. Gemma

GEMMA. Do you prefer it peeled, is that it?

HOLLY. I'm not, to be honest it's making me gag a little, just smelling it.

GEMMA. What if I juiced it instead?

Might be easier to stomach.

HOLLY. I really

GEMMA *gets a few more oranges from the fridge.*

Sit down, Gemma, you're not here to wait on me.

GEMMA. Don't be silly.

GEMMA *halves the oranges.*

Where's your juicer?

HOLLY. If you're making it for yourself that's fine. Bottom cupboard.

GEMMA *gets out the juicer.*

GEMMA (*while she squeezes the oranges*). We should do some light exercise. I know you're not up to much, but you could show me what you do in your antenatal classes. I've always been intrigued, but you can't just go along on your own, can you, if you're not pregnant.

HOLLY. I might just get some sleep.

You don't have to stay.

GEMMA. What would Greg think if I left?

HOLLY. It's funny, Monique said she was free.

GEMMA. Something must've come up.

HOLLY. Guess so.

Pause.

GEMMA. You like her then, Monique?

HOLLY. Yes.

GEMMA. Always seems a bit cold, but maybe that's just me.

HOLLY. She's not.

GEMMA. Must be me then.

She pours the freshly squeezed orange juice into a glass.

Hopefully this'll be a bit more palatable for you.

GEMMA *holds out the glass to* HOLLY.

HOLLY. Honestly, Gemma, I'm not feeling

GEMMA. It's a glass of juice, it's a simple glass of juice.

HOLLY. Oranges are one of the things I'm finding it hard to

GEMMA. It's health in a glass, Holly. Right here.

One sip. That's all I'm asking.

She holds out the glass.

HOLLY *takes it.*

She holds it up to her mouth, but gags.

It's not as if you're allergic. It's not going to hurt you, it's in your head.

HOLLY. I can't.

GEMMA (*takes the glass*). Oh for God's sake.

She downs the juice.

Delicious.

She starts to wash up the glass, juicer and knife.

HOLLY. You don't have to do that.

GEMMA. Of course I do, I'm the one made the mess.

HOLLY. I'm sorry.

GEMMA. What for?

HOLLY. Give it a couple of months and I'm sure I'll be eating everything in sight. I'll be huge.

GEMMA *finishes washing up*.

GEMMA (*drying up*). Before you get too big

(*Holds up the glass*.) Are these new?

HOLLY. No.

GEMMA. Don't recognise them, where are they from?

HOLLY. Can't remember.

GEMMA (*putting the glass away*). Before the baby

We should do something.

HOLLY. Like what?

GEMMA. We never did climb Everest for my fiftieth.

HOLLY. We had a party.

GEMMA. Oh I'm not complaining, I'll never forget that. But that's what I mean, we should do something we'll never forget.

HOLLY. Everest?

GEMMA. Doesn't have to be a mountain, could be closer to home, could be

You never did cross the desert. For example.

We could do that.

HOLLY. While I'm pregnant?

GEMMA. As you said, you'll start to feel better soon. It doesn't have to incapacitate you for the entire nine months.

HOLLY. I still have to be careful.

Crossing a desert isn't exactly

Are you serious?

GEMMA. Why not?

HOLLY. The tiny distance between my air-conditioned car and an air-conditioned building fills me with dread and you're talking about walking out into an oven.

GEMMA. What happened to you?

HOLLY. I'm having a baby, Gemma.

GEMMA. You wanted to cross that desert more than anything. That's why you came out here isn't it? It's your reason for being here.

HOLLY. Not any more.

GEMMA. Did it just disappear? That desire, that need, that was so strong you risked your life to

HOLLY. I risked my life, exactly. I'm not doing that again.

GEMMA. You wouldn't be. We'd do it together. It wouldn't be nearly as dangerous.

HOLLY. No.

I mean, I still don't know if you're a hundred percent serious, but just to be clear, absolutely not, no.

Put your energies into planning a baby shower, if you want, even though the thought of that is only marginally less painful than walking out into a desert.

GEMMA. Another party.

HOLLY. If you must.

GEMMA. I don't want another party.

HOLLY. Good, because I was already regretting even mentioning that.

Pause.

GEMMA. We're both in good shape, Holly.

HOLLY. I can hold my own in a boxfit class, that does not mean I should be crossing the hottest place on earth.

GEMMA. Not cross its entirety, that might be pushing it, you're right. But a section, a stretch, enough to push us, not kill us.

HOLLY. Leave it, Gemma.

Pause.

GEMMA. Tala begged me not to let her go. Did I tell you that?

HOLLY. No, you didn't.

GEMMA. It was terrible. Really hard. Genuinely.

She was like a sister. Even though our conversations were
limited, because of the language, she'd been with us for
years, and when you see someone day in day out you don't
have to speak the same language to understand one another.
In fact she begged me in Filipino, but I knew exactly what
she was saying.

It never gets easier.

But Patrick's the sensible one, the one with the business
brain, and times like these, he said, you can't afford to be
sentimental. Never can, really.

You're about to embark on this whole new adventure, but
before that, let's do this one thing, Holly.

Don't make me beg.

You're getting on here, making a life for yourself, and I
know you weren't sure at first, but turns out you're the lucky
ones after all, because there's nothing going back home. Ask
Darren. Ask anyone.

Don't make me

Scene Two

The same apartment. HOLLY *and* GREG.

GREG. You're scared of her.

HOLLY. I'm not.

GREG. I don't blame you.

HOLLY. I'm not scared of her, don't say that.

GREG. You probably should be.

HOLLY. She's only

GREG. I think we've been pretty amenable, haven't we?

HOLLY. Yes.

GREG. I think we've been pretty fucking tolerant, all things considered.

HOLLY. Yes, Greg, we have.

GREG. So she can just fuck right off. You're not going.

Pause.

HOLLY. I don't want to go.

GREG. You don't have to. Case closed.

HOLLY. But

GREG *shakes his head.*

GREG. It's not just you now, Holly.

HOLLY. Listen to me.

GREG. You said you'd never go out there again.

HOLLY. I know what I said.

GREG. You promised.

That was an important promise, Holly. A really important promise.

HOLLY. I know what I promised, and I don't want to go out there, believe me.

GREG. You're not going out there.

HOLLY. But I wonder

GREG. No.

HOLLY. Just hear me out.

GREG. It's non-negotiable.

HOLLY. It might be a good idea.

GREG. That's our child. Not yours. Ours.

HOLLY. Will you listen?

GREG. I don't need to. Not to this.

HOLLY. If I do this

GREG. No.

HOLLY. If I do

GREG. No.

HOLLY. If

GREG. No.

HOLLY. Greg.

Pause.

This really isn't about me testing myself, or searching for something or

I understand why you think it is, but if I was doing it for those reasons

Would I tell you? Would I be talking to you about this?

GREG. So you're telling me you're doing this?

HOLLY. No, Greg, I'm telling you what Gemma said. I'm talking to you about it. I've come to you. To talk about it. So can we do that, at least?

GREG. I told you, it's non-negotiable.

HOLLY. This is completely different to before.

GREG. Is it?

Because it looks the same to me. You. In a desert. Risking your life. Two lives, this time. So I suppose it is different. Worse.

HOLLY. I just think if I do this, then Gemma, she might

GREG. She'll never be satisfied, you know that, don't you?

You can do this and any other crazy challenge she comes up with but she'll always want more.

HOLLY. I don't think so.

GREG. You're scared to say no.

HOLLY. I'm not.

GREG. But there's a limit and, we've put up with a lot but, this is the limit now, that's it.

Pause.

Did you speak to Monique?

HOLLY. No.

GREG. You didn't ask her if she really was busy this morning?

HOLLY. I haven't had a chance / to

GREG. Of course she wasn't.

HOLLY. It's possible.

GREG. You only arranged it yesterday.

HOLLY. Things come up.

GREG. It was Gemma.

HOLLY. Okay, Greg. Maybe it was.

GREG. It was.

Pause.

Look, tell her it's me. Tell her I won't let you. That's the truth, anyway.

Tell her the doctor won't allow it. Ruled it out immediately. Because she would. Don't even need to ask. Anyone, I mean, anyone can see that it'd be crazy for a pregnant woman to go out there. Don't need to be a medical professional.

Pause.

HOLLY. Might be a good way to draw a line, doing this with her might, in some way, I don't know, it just feels like if we went out there together, she'd be

GREG. For all I know, Holly, for all I know, she's taking my wife, and my unborn child / into

HOLLY. Our child.

GREG. Our unborn child, into the middle of nowhere, to I don't know, bludgeon you to death.

HOLLY *laughs.*

Don't laugh.

HOLLY. Bludgeon me, is that

To death. What?

GREG. Do not laugh.

HOLLY. Bludgeon me to death.

GREG. Well if she doesn't get you the heat will, it's the same outcome in the end.

HOLLY. I think she just wants an adventure. To feel, like we've shared something, I don't know.

I don't think she wants to kill me.

Silence.

I don't want to go out there.

GREG. We're doing alright, you and me.

HOLLY. We have to live with these people. We have to get along.

GREG. We do get along.

That doesn't mean pandering to her every crazy whim.

Pause.

HOLLY. Darren never said goodbye.

GREG. No, well

Scene Three

PATRICK *and* GEMMA*'s apartment.* PATRICK *sits drinking a Bloody Mary.* GEMMA *is searching through the kitchen drawers for a ladle.*

GEMMA. Don't know where anything is in my own kitchen, it's disgraceful.

PATRICK. Just order something in. They won't mind.

GEMMA. I've spent all afternoon preparing this, Patrick.

PATRICK. Smells delicious by the way.

GEMMA. Takeaways aren't cheap.

PATRICK. Have to eat.

GEMMA. Times like these a bit of home cooking's not a bad idea, that's all.

Anyway, you don't invite people for dinner and serve them takeaway.

PATRICK. I don't invite people for dinner at all.

Don't know why you did. See Greg all day.

GEMMA *takes the casserole dish out of the oven.*

What is it?

GEMMA. Irish stew.

PATRICK. Haven't had that in

Can't remember when.

My favourite.

GEMMA. I know.

PATRICK. Smells delicious.

GEMMA. Nice to do some cooking.

PATRICK. No complaints from me.

GEMMA. I'd forgotten.

She stirs the stew.

Spoke to Tala.

Her English is even worse on the phone.

Her new people are French so she's not hearing it as much I suppose.

Barely managed a few minutes.

PATRICK. At least she found something.

GEMMA. She said they're good people.

But she wouldn't complain, even if they weren't.

PATRICK. I'm sure they're treating her well.

GEMMA. They were probably in the same room, I mean, what's she going to say.

PATRICK. There's no reason to think they're not treating her well, Gemma.

Pause.

We just didn't need her.

And you enjoy cooking, anyway. You're good at it.

GEMMA *sets the table.*

GEMMA. I'm sorry you have to see Greg. Been with him all day.

PATRICK. It's alright.

GEMMA. Must be sick of each other.

Last thing you want's to come home and

PATRICK. It's alright, Gemma. Really.

PATRICK *gets up and heads to the bathroom.*

GEMMA. Where are you going?

PATRICK. The shower.

GEMMA. There's no time.

PATRICK. I'll be / quick.

GEMMA. There's no time, Patrick.

PATRICK. There's time for a shower.

GEMMA. I need you to help me.

PATRICK. With what?

GEMMA. Set the table.

PATRICK. I've had a long day, Gemma, you've invited people over, fine, but I need to

GEMMA *stands between* PATRICK *and the bathroom door.*

You're blocking my way?

GEMMA. You don't smell.

PATRICK. Thank you but I still want a shower.

GEMMA. Have one later.

PATRICK. Is there something in there you don't want me to see?

GEMMA *kisses* PATRICK, *he pulls away.*

Christ, must be serious, what've you done?

GEMMA. Can't I kiss you?

PATRICK. Is it a dead body or something?

GEMMA. Can't I kiss my husband without it being some suspicious act, some cover-up. A dead body?

PATRICK. It was a joke, Gemma, don't get / all

GEMMA. When did a kiss become so rare that you think it /
    must be

PATRICK. It's not rare. We kiss.

    Pause.

GEMMA. What are we doing here?

PATRICK. Right now? Right now I'd like to be having a
    shower.

GEMMA. There's no work.

PATRICK. There's work.

GEMMA. Twenty-five years. We've been here twenty-five
    years, working, and I'm not going to lose it all now because
    you can't see when to quit.

PATRICK. Quit?

GEMMA. It's not your fault, the work just isn't there.

PATRICK. Didn't realise I've been married to a business expert
    all these years.

GEMMA. Retire early. Isn't that what we've been working for?

PATRICK. We?

    Pause.

GEMMA. I can't watch while everything we've worked for,
    everything we've built up, gets eaten away.

PATRICK. Have I ever let you down?

    Gemma?

GEMMA. No.

PATRICK. Okay then.

    Pause.

GEMMA. You've worked hard. And I'm proud of you. Don't
    throw it away. It hasn't come easy, so let's not waste it.

    I could let you pretend everything's fine. But it's not.

PATRICK. What do you know?

GEMMA. You only have to turn on the news / to see

PATRICK. Oh, I see, so that's where this expertise is coming from. CNN.

GEMMA. So what are you telling me, you've got plenty of work?

PATRICK. Enough.

GEMMA *shakes her head.*

I'm not oblivious, Gemma, to the current

The economic situation.

The global financial

The crisis.

I'm not burying my head in the fucking desert, okay, I let Darren go, didn't I? Jeff. Nick. Fifteen years he'd been with me, I make the tough decisions when I have to, so do not come to / me and

GEMMA. Now. You have to now.

PATRICK. What about Greg?

Au revoir. Auf Wiedersehen. Good fucking luck. That how you treat your friends?

GEMMA. Are they friends?

PATRICK. You're the one invited them for dinner, you tell me.

GEMMA. I don't know.

PATRICK. Why'd you invite them then?

GEMMA. I don't know.

PATRICK. Well that's just

Pause.

PATRICK *goes into the bathroom.*

Pause.

The sound of the shower.

GEMMA *goes to the table. She folds, and refolds the napkins.*

She lays out the glasses.

She opens a bottle of wine and pours herself a glass.

The sound of the shower stops. She watches the door.

PATRICK *enters in a bathrobe. He sits on the sofa and starts reading the paper.*

Pause.

GEMMA. Are you going to get dressed?

Pause.

They'd be fine. He's well-qualified. He'd find another job.

PATRICK. How?

If there's no work, as you say.

GEMMA. That's not really your

Pause.

I know it's not nice letting someone go.

PATRICK. How many people have you fired?

GEMMA. I spoke to Tala. That wasn't easy.

PATRICK. Alan Sugar eat your heart out.

GEMMA. Look I'm not claiming to be

This isn't about Greg, that's a side issue, I'm talking about our future / here.

PATRICK. Is that why you invited them over?

GEMMA. What?

PATRICK. To fire him? Pass the salt oh and by the way you're fired.

GEMMA. No.

PATRICK. You're asking me, but if I won't, you'll go ahead and do it anyway.

GEMMA. I'm not asking you to fire him, I'm asking you to consider, to think about finishing up here while we've still got something.

We could buy a boat, a yacht, go sailing. There are so many things we could do. We could buy a cottage back home, somewhere green and wet and go for long bracing walks in the cold. We could visit everyone we've met, all over the world, South America, Canada, Russia.

PATRICK. You think they remember you?

GEMMA. We knew some of them for years, of course they

Every email Gabi writes she says to go and visit them in Brazil.

PATRICK. Gabi?

GEMMA. Gabi. Gabi and Luis.

You remember them, they only left, well, it was probably ten years ago now, but we had dinner with them every night for almost two years, you used to go to the races with Luis, he was from Argentina, remember, he knew a lot about horses, grew up on some kind of ranch.

You do remember.

You would if you saw them. I've got photos.

PATRICK. I don't need photos.

GEMMA (*searching for the album*). He's incredibly handsome. Looks like Jonny Wilkinson.

PATRICK. Oh, I remember now.

GEMMA. Really?

PATRICK. No.

GEMMA. They're both beautiful in fact, she's typically Brazilian.

I know I've got photos, I threw Gabi a surprise birthday party at Uptown, we took loads on the terrace at sunset.

PATRICK. I believe you, I believe we knew them.

GEMMA. You must remember them.

She goes into the spare room.

PATRICK. You don't have to tear the place apart.

GEMMA (*from the spare room*). They'll be in the wardrobe.

PATRICK. Thought they were in Brazil.

GEMMA (*from the spare room*). The photos.

Pause.

PATRICK. Was he in telecommunications?

GEMMA. He worked for, yeah, he worked for some phone company, you see, you do remember him.

PATRICK. Mystery solved.

GEMMA *enters, flicking through a photo album.*

Mystery solved, Gemma, you don't need / to

GEMMA. I haven't looked at these in years.

(*Points at a photo.*) Do you remember them? Mattias and Kim.

PATRICK. I'm not playing this game.

GEMMA. Bit full of themselves. Had the most obnoxious kids.

PATRICK. So why keep photos of them?

GEMMA. Where are you, Gabi?

PATRICK. I don't want to be on holiday for the rest of my life. Visiting people I barely remember.

GEMMA. Look, here they are. (*Shows him a picture.*) That was her birthday. How beautiful are they? Sickening.

PATRICK. What would we talk about with these people?

GEMMA. What do we talk about with anyone?

Look it was just an example. Gabi and Luis. We don't have to visit them.

PATRICK. And where's all this money coming from? Jetting across the world. Yachts. Who do you think we are?

GEMMA. You're successful, Patrick.

PATRICK. I'm no Alan Sugar.

GEMMA. You've never let me down.

PATRICK. And I'm not going to start now.

I know you worry but you really don't have to.

Don't watch the news, it's

GEMMA. It's not the news.

PATRICK. Things aren't easy at the moment, for anyone, sure, but in a couple of years

Greg's turned out to be a real asset, people like him, there's potential there to

GEMMA. You think he won't leave you the first chance he gets?

The doorbell.

They have no interest in us, Patrick, you and me, they have no desire to

PATRICK. Are you going to get that?

Pause.

PATRICK *picks up the entryphone.*

Hello. Come in.

He buzzes them in.

They're here, aren't they?

GEMMA *goes to the oven and takes out a tray of hors d'oeuvres. She slides them onto a plate, paying no attention to presentation.*

They didn't have to come.

A knock on the door.

Pause.

PATRICK *answers the door.*

HOLLY. Nice to see you've dressed up for the occasion.

PATRICK. Thought I'd make the effort, you know.

In you come then.

They enter.

It's been too long, Greg, far too long.

GREG. It's nice to see you away from the office. Hi, Gemma.

GEMMA. Greg.

Holly. How're you feeling?

HOLLY. Yeah, you know.

GEMMA. No. That's why I'm asking.

HOLLY. I'm, good, yeah I'm feeling okay. Thank you.

GREG. Past the sick phase now I think, aren't we?

GEMMA. We? Were you sick too, Greg?

GREG. No, no. Holly's the one that's been, but

PATRICK. Holly's been sick but you've both been suffering, right?

GREG. No, she hasn't complained at all.

I bet women hate that, don't they, when men say we, we're having a baby, we've been sick, we

GEMMA. I don't know. Do you, Holly?

HOLLY. It's not really something that

GEMMA. You're feeling stronger now. That's the main thing.

HOLLY. Yeah. I don't want to push it, but, I think so.

PATRICK. Drink?

GREG. Yeah, a beer.

PATRICK. Done. And I think we've got, what've we got in terms of non-alcoholic options, Gemma?

GEMMA. Water.

PATRICK. Sparkling or

GEMMA. Flat.

PATRICK. That's it?

GEMMA. Everything seemed to be making you sick. I didn't
want to force anything on you. Anything too full of flavour or

HOLLY. Water's perfect, thank you.

PATRICK. Rather you than me, but water it is.

*He goes to the fridge and takes two beers and a bottle of
water. He pours a glass of water.*

GREG. Smells delicious, what is it?

GEMMA. Irish stew.

GREG. My favourite.

GEMMA. Everyone's favourite apparently.

Hope it won't be too much for you, Holly. But I thought it

HOLLY. It's perfect.

GEMMA. You haven't tasted it yet.

GREG. Well it smells great.

PATRICK (*handing* HOLLY *and* GREG *their drinks*). She's a
good cook, my wife.

GEMMA. Well, haven't killed anyone yet I suppose.

She holds out the plate of hors d'oeuvres.

Mushrooms are okay I hope.

HOLLY. Yeah, great.

Takes one.

GREG (*takes one*). Thanks.

GEMMA. Couldn't get the right cheese so they're probably a bit

GREG. Hot but

HOLLY. They're really good.

GREG. Nothing beats a bit of proper home cooking.

GEMMA. Times like these

PATRICK. We're not on the breadline, Gemma.

Cheers.

GREG. Cheers.

They drink. GEMMA *sips her wine.*

HOLLY. It's not a special occasion is it? Dinner.

PATRICK. Don't need a reason do we? To eat together.

GREG. No, but we were trying to remember, it's not a birthday or anything, is it? Didn't want you thinking we'd forgotten.

GEMMA. Well technically you didn't remember so

PATRICK. People make such a fuss about these things, it's dinner, that's all, nothing special.

GEMMA. Couple of years' time you'll have forgotten it ever happened.

PATRICK. Well that's

GEMMA. It's true. Couple of years' time you'll have a child, you'll be wherever you are and we'll be wherever we are and it'll be as if it never happened.

Pause.

HOLLY. We brought a present. Just in case.

She gets a bottle of champagne out of her bag.

PATRICK. That's very / generous.

HOLLY. Generic. I know, but we weren't sure, so

Here.

PATRICK *takes it.*

PATRICK. Thank you. Cristal, very nice.

GREG. Actually since it's not a birthday that's good, cos we were wondering if you'd mind making it an early one.

PATRICK. You only just got here.

GREG. Oh I know, we're not leaving yet, just

GEMMA. We won't keep you.

HOLLY. Don't be silly, / we're

GEMMA. Silly?

HOLLY. We're not rushing off.

GEMMA. Another party?

GREG. It's a work thing, really. Monique, Chris's wife

GEMMA. I know Monique.

GREG. Right, of course, well it's her birthday.

HOLLY. We might not go, Greg told them it'd depend how I felt, but

GREG. It's just I don't think it'd hurt, to pop in, show our faces.

I didn't realise this had been organised, when I said I'd go.

PATRICK. It's fine.

GREG. It's work, really.

GEMMA. You said.

GREG. Chris is a good client, and they're doing well, can't hurt / to

PATRICK. Hear that? They're doing well.

GEMMA (*takes bottle from* PATRICK). You should give this to her.

GREG. No, no, that's for you.

GEMMA. No, you should give it to Monique. It's her birthday.

HOLLY. It's for you, Gemma.

GEMMA. But it wasn't. It was for me or Patrick, depending on the occasion.

PATRICK. I'm very happy to keep it, in fact let's open it now.

GEMMA. Why? Are we celebrating?

PATRICK. Well, potentially.

GEMMA. He's attending a birthday party, Patrick, that's hardly a guaranteed contract.

GREG. We've just opened our beers anyway, so

GEMMA. Exactly, shouldn't be wasteful, times like these.

(*Offers* HOLLY *the plate*.) Mushroom thing?

HOLLY *takes one*.

PATRICK. Still, it sounds promising. And he likes you, Chris, didn't I tell you? Has he said anything more specific, about their plans, when / they might

HOLLY. No business talk.

GEMMA. What would you rather talk about, Holly?

The weather?

It's hot.

PATRICK. He loved that interior designer you got for him, the Australian. Takes time, that's what I'm always telling people, but you work on these relationships, you go to the wife's birthday parties, and it pays off eventually.

HOLLY. I like Monique. I'm going for her.

GEMMA. Of course.

PATRICK. But it doesn't hurt, that's what I'm saying. Put in the time.

GEMMA. And we're speaking from experience, because hell, we've done the time.

PATRICK. Right, shall we eat?

GEMMA. They've got to get off.

HOLLY. There's no rush.

GEMMA. Still.

GEMMA *takes four bowls from the cupboard and ladles the stew into the bowls*.

HOLLY. Let me help.

GEMMA. You can cut the bread if you want.

GREG. Going dune bashing, did I mention, couple of guys from Campbell's.

PATRICK. Campbell's?

Two conversations continue simultaneously (the starred lines are spoken at the same time).

* HOLLY. How thick? This okay?

GEMMA. Whatever you want.

HOLLY (*cutting the bread*). Didn't know you enjoyed cooking.

We don't even own any pots. If I wanted to cook anything I'd have to go and buy them especially, which makes it, I mean obviously it's possible, it just makes it more of an ordeal, but I suppose with the baby I suppose I'll become more of a homemaker, but I think you're either like that or not.

It's healthier though, cooking, isn't it, you can watch what's going in, much better.

GEMMA. I've been wanting to ask

HOLLY. Yeah.

GEMMA. Did you want to kill yourself?

HOLLY. What?

* GREG. Next week. Invited me along, thought it couldn't hurt.

PATRICK. Right.

GREG. What?

PATRICK. No, just they've got their own HR department, I mean, they don't usually hire in specialists all that much.

GREG. Probably just being friendly. Bit of a jolly, isn't it.

If you wanted to come along, I'm sure they'd love to / have you.

PATRICK. Not really my thing.

GREG. No, which is what they figured, I guess. Not really my thing, to be honest, bit nervous.

PATRICK. What's to be nervous about?

GREG. Can get a bit competitive, these things, can't they. No one wants to lose.

PATRICK. No one wants to look stupid.

GREG. Everyone's trying to impress. It's supposed to be fun, but

PATRICK. You're good at these kinds of things.

GREG. I don't know, I don't really like it out there, to be honest, get a bit

PATRICK. What are you talking about, Gemma?

GEMMA. In the desert.

Did you?

GREG. Did she what?

PATRICK (*putting the bowls on the table*). Everyone's hungry, Gemma, they just want to eat.

GEMMA. I wouldn't judge you. And I wouldn't gossip. Whatever you might think.

PATRICK. You don't have to answer. I'm sorry, Holly, it's completely

I don't know what she's talking about.

GEMMA. Holly does.

GREG. What?

GEMMA. The desert.

GREG. What about it?

GEMMA. I helped you lie to Greg.

PATRICK. Sit down, Holly, let's eat.

HOLLY. Why are you asking? Why's it even matter?

GEMMA. I drove you out there.

GREG. When?

HOLLY. When we first got here, years ago, I don't know why / she's

PATRICK. Please sit, everyone.

HOLLY. I really don't understand why you're so, why it matters so much to you.

GEMMA. At the time I thought to myself, look, she barely knows you, you can't expect her to pour her heart out, so I didn't take it personally, that you wouldn't talk to me / that was normal.

HOLLY. I talked to you.

GEMMA. That was normal, you're English, I didn't expect anything else, but now, I thought now it might be alright to ask.

PATRICK. At dinner?

GEMMA. Was I wrong? Because that was years ago, as you say. But now, we're connected I thought.

GREG. Connected?

HOLLY. Some things are private, don't you think?

PATRICK. Of course they are.

GREG. Holly has no obligation to share anything with you. That wasn't in the contract.

GEMMA. I'm not demanding anything, I'm just asking.

PATRICK. Look, let's sit down and eat.

Holly was right, no business talk, contracts and

This is dinner.

GREG. I have business dinners all the time.

PATRICK. Well this isn't one of them.

GEMMA. It was just a question. There's no contractual duty to answer it. No expectation that you will. I'd be surprised if you did.

Pause.

GEMMA *sits down and starts eating. The others sit.*

HOLLY. I didn't want to kill myself.

GEMMA. Then why were you going out there all the time?

PATRICK. She answered your question, Gemma.

GEMMA. I just want to understand. Because it feels like I knew you just as well then as I do now, as if the years in between have meant nothing, might as well have not happened, and that shouldn't be how it works, should it?

PATRICK. Interrogating people's not how it works.

GEMMA. Am I interrogating you?

Pause.

You don't have to answer. I thought that was clear.

PATRICK *eats.*

PATRICK. Careful, it's hot.

They all eat.

GREG. Really good.

GEMMA. I wasn't interrogating you, Holly.

PATRICK. Alright, Gemma.

GEMMA. I won't go on about it, I just want you to know that.

HOLLY. There's no big secret, Gemma.

They eat in silence.

PATRICK *pours water for himself,* GREG *and* GEMMA.

PATRICK. This thing with Campbell's

They just contact you? Out of the blue.

GREG. I know a couple of guys there. From Sevens.

PATRICK. Oh right.

GREG. They just thought I'd enjoy it I think.

PATRICK. Help yourself to bread.

GREG *and* HOLLY *take a slice.*

GREG. Like you said, put in the time.

PATRICK *nods*.

They eat.

Silence.

HOLLY. Mum used to say it's a good sign. If you can be silent with someone.

Sign of a good

A good thing.

We never talked much, we'd be together, but we'd just

They eat in silence.

ENVELOPE
CALEDAR